The Silence of the Church:
The Spiritual Struggle with Sexuality

James McReynolds
Minister of Joy to the World

Parson's Porch
Book Publishing

The Silence of the Church: The Spiritual Struggle with Sexuality
ISBN: Softcover 978-1-946478-38-2
Copyright © 2017 by James McReynolds

All rights reserved. No part of this book may be reproduced or transmitted in any form or by any means, electronic or mechanical, including photocopying, recording, or by any information storage and retrieval system, without permission in writing from the publisher.

To order additional copies of this book, contact:

Parson's Porch Books
1-423-475-7308
www.parsonsporch.com

Parson's Porch Books is an imprint of **Parson's Porch & Book Publishers** in Cleveland, Tennessee, which has double focus. We focus on the needs of creative writers who need a professional publisher to get their work to market, & we also focus on the needs of others by sharing our profits with those who struggle in poverty to meet their basic needs of food, clothing, shelter and safety.

The Silence of the Church

Dedication

In loving memory of

Lena Mae Reynolds

My mom who inspired me for a lifetime

Other Books by James E. McReynolds
published by Parson's Porch Books

The Spirituality of Joy: The Least Discussed Human Emotion the

Joy of Preaching: Encountering Jesus Through the Word of God

Dancing with God: A Theology of Joy

Contents

Foreword by AJ Beaber..10

Passionate Love and the Silence of the Church the Spiritual Struggle with Sexuality..13

Breaking the Silence About Our Sexual Selves....................19

What Do We Mean When We Say, "I Love You?"..........26

Let Us Rejoice and Be Glad in It.......................................32

It's Time to Have the Talk with the Church......................39

How Did I Get to Be 75 When I Feel Like 25? 47

The Silence and the Shame of Sexual Violence in the Church.......57

He Had Sex with Someone Else..65

Silence and the Continuing Sexual Revolution..................74

Has God Picked Someone Special for Me to Marry?.......80

Feeling Life: Sexuality and Joy..88

"The Word Became Flesh"..95

Positive Messages the Church Needs to Share on Sexuality........ 104

Jesus Ministered to All People.. 113

Practical Applications 120

Afterword by John Killinger... 125

Acknowledgments 125

Foreword

The church is a congregation of likeminded believers, supporting and encouraging one another; a place of forgiveness and healing. On any given Sunday, you will find pastors speaking passionately from the pulpit, people singing and worshiping unashamed of their love for God. Yet mention the word "sex" or "sexuality" and you can hear a pin drop.

Why the silence around the topic of sexuality in the church? Where did the passion go? Where did the celebration of lovers, like the teaching on the subject from the Songs of Solomon go?

This book is a bold proclamation, from a courageous pastor, willing to break the silence and speak about the joy still found in sexuality and the church. It challenges congregations everywhere to open their platforms and ministries to discuss this important subject; one that deeply affects our households and future generations.

Here one will discover a voice for sexuality from a spiritual perspective, filled with love and grace, giving us permission to fully embrace our sexuality as a gift from God.

Thank you pastor James for your courage to share.

AJ Beaber

Introduction

Passionate Love and the Silence of the Church the Spiritual Struggle with Sexuality

The sound of silence is the easy way to approach the human struggle with sexuality. Churches can create an atmosphere that it is soul-healing to talk about everything else, but not about "that." Many congregations are saying by this attitude that church is not a safe place to talk about our sexual selves.

Fear and shame heads up the reasons church leaders act out of knowing nothing to do.

During our Spiritual Visionquests for Joy, we run into many roadblocks. One would think church people would eagerly ask for help to bring the light of the gospel of grace and love. In my experience, they will not be open to it. In churches of almost every denomination, I have led Family Life retreats or conferences on family issues. Some ask me to come back every year. Issues such as finances, communication, fidelity, self-esteem, raising children or stress reduction, or the hurtful consequences of adultery or abuse. Sexuality is still a taboo subject.

Yet there is no marriage without sexual intercourse. Marriage became a sacrament in the teaching of early churches. Partners were fully married while they were still virgins. In our marriage ceremony, we vow spiritual sexual intimacy.

The silence of the church is crippling family life. As Genesis 4:7 declares, "Sin is crouching at the door and its desire is to have you." People are starving for love, for comfort, for relief, and happiness and times of joy in living as a sexual self.

As you look at the people coming to worship, more than you can realize are struggling with routine and stress. Adult videos, internet, movies and dating or match-making sights are enabling sexual desires and frustrations, offering relief from loneliness, and personal struggles.

Those who are in control of the life and communication will go to any length to show that the gospel has no practical answers. Filled with fear, shame, and hatred of self and others who may be different in their views.

Sexuality is not a major theme of Scripture. It does give light on living our brief days of our human journey. The Word persuades us that we are body as well as soul. We are not searching for sexual information. We are creating a vision that is informed by God's guidance.

Some school-based sex education classes presume that relationships between the genders is genital in nature. Relationships that begin with sex, ends in dissatisfaction and pain. The church must offer the means of grace.

So, our congregations remain silent. Ministers today, even younger highly trained ones, do not deeply believe that the message of the gospel can transform deep sexual struggles with "the joy of the Lord." The Bible is not a shy, silent guide about our sexual self and about brokenness through our decisions concerning sex. God is not surprised. God responds with grace, and so should we. The spiritual struggle with sexuality is an ongoing battle.

Many congregations remain silent because there is unresolved sexual baggage that brings deep shame.

Shame thrives on secret keeping. As one of my licensed mental health practitioners said, "We are only as sick as our secrets. "In my own ministry of psychotherapy, I found people who struggled with unhappiness would share their secrets with me as a professional therapist than as a pastor. When people shared their trauma stories, mental, spiritual, and physical health improved and they lived with less stress.

Shame is the fear of disconnection. Often this must do with power and control. Vulnerable people fear that they are unlovable and do not belong. Some tend to over focus on their children's lives, work, addictions, and affairs. Shame keeps us from being intimate with each other and being vulnerable as an individual or a group is the healing path and courage is the light.

We can never create a new past. Failures from our past that involve a powerful experience such as sex haunts many people for years. We cannot be vulnerable and intimate if we play those unhappy experiences in the tapes of our minds which continue in the present time to keep people from being available to those living in shame. Those ongoing struggles fill us with a pervasive gloom of shame, and our conscience freezes us into inaction.

This is a huge road block to teaching and communicating to our kids and young people about sex in a redemptive way. So, the church is frozen from offering our youth decent exposure concerning sexuality. Parents carry around unresolved sexual sin struggles in their souls and minds. They can be issues from long ago or in current struggles.

Churches and leaders who join what I call the Joy Movement must have courage to minister to those scarred by and struggling with sexual issues. Ministers must provide a context, a place where people can have a framework for discovering that God in Christ can bring wholeness, healing, and growth.

Jesus spoke at the time of the anointing tears of the sinful woman at his feet, "He (or she) who has been forgiven much, loves much." See Luke 7:36-50. Our appreciation for "the joy of the Lord" in our salvation leads us to discover and be available to minister to others, even if their struggles and temptations are different from our own sins. This insight will cause us to be trained to be better help and support.

God highly desires to meet people in the middle of their problems, to bring them life, joy, and wholeness. The church is still God's chosen instrument for the transformation of each person, all nations and all cultures.

Congregations remain silent because people distrust sex as being good. This book is not about how to assume the best sexual positions or to create an atmosphere that enhances sexual joy. The goal of this book is to illuminate what has been so assiduously avoided in these impersonal and sterile works concerning "Christian" sex. We can tell who we are and what we believe by seeing how we act, dream, think, and feel sexually. We can make healthy changes based on what we understand. We express our fundamental natures through our choices involving sex.

We must talk to our children and youth about trust and body contact. When trust is violated or body contact unreliable for comfort, as children we develop defenses against being hurt. Too much in today's atmosphere presents sex in a negative or broken sense that we have stopped believing sex was meant for our highest good, or that God desires us to experience being a sexual being as something full of joy.

Somehow the churches and ministers need to proclaim the goodness of God's gift of sexuality. We need to affirm God's good intention for it. Sex can be a soul-uniting force between two committed people. Passionate sexes so beyond just pleasurable that it is wonderfully addictive.

Few sermons boldly show that "The Song of Songs" belongs in our Holy Scriptures where on every page we understand God's design and the beauty of sexuality.

We transfer our own attitudes about sex to our children. In today's church climate, when and if there is talk about sex, the church teaches only how it has gone wrong. They attempt to warn children and youth into obedience and doing what is the correct thing.

I am grateful to the many churches that have trusted me to bring God's plan for love. I stand and meditate in awe that "the joy the Lord is our strength." Not my insights or experiences in counseling thousands of people, but Christ living in me gives me the authority to communicate on what real love is. One of my books on joy is titled: *Passionate Joy: Building a Wealth of Joy in a World Starved for Love.*

What a privilege to be chosen to participate in the work of the Kingdom bringing salvation to the world through Christ. Much of this material was shared with youth and adults of every generation in Visionquests for Joy. We certainly need to know how to date well, so that we do marriage well. We need to know how to break the silence to proclaim the realm of our everyday lives. Other people are traveling the same roads that we are.

This message has broken the silence. The harvest is plenty. People of all ages are starved for this message. They want some trusted guidance. They are starved for God's love.

The evaluations from my communications reflect joy, wonder, and insight. Far too many struggling people want me to address their pain. Diverse people of all ages and cultures in all areas of the nation and in all the countries and territories I have been privileged to visit ask the same questions. We all struggle with the same problems and challenges.

Every human on their brief earthly journey have two fears. We fear not being loved. And we also feel fear of not being able to give love. To desire to be loved is not wrong. We were made to love. We have a deep desire to connect with others. We need people around us who will be there for us no matter what comes or goes. God is love. And God's created people are designed for love.

We stay alone and silent, partly because it is so difficult to be clearly communicated with grace and compassion. Confusion is ignited when people talk about love. This is also a mystery when some person says that they love you. How and in what way do they love you? And we reflect on how we know true love.

Confused and struggling people go off to find themselves. They might quit their jobs and go away to find "where the joy is."

Few "find themselves" through self-centered introspection. Isolating ourselves or traveling to an exotic location will not create happiness. The road to knowing deep joy and lasting happiness is to give ourselves away. Our loving actions show we care and desire for others that they become the best versions of themselves.

James McReynolds

Regardless of the circumstances, there is joy and satisfaction in helping others that far surpasses any inconvenience we might experience in the process.

Flourishing lives come by joining our lives and our needs to those of others, and in living a life of interdependence, knowing that we are willing to look out for the good of others.

This book can be used as a resource for community or faith groups.

Chapter One

Breaking the Silence About Our Sexual Selves

God invented sex. Our culture is dominated by sex, but often cheapens it. The Church frequently presents unhelpful views on sex, but we are certainly sexual beings, fearfully and wonderfully made. God designed female and male bodies to fit together perfectly as one flesh. There is nothing shameful about our sexuality. God created sex and meant it to be good. Sex is for bonding, reproduction, and pleasure.

Sex is a marvelous way to express love and deep commitment for one another. Humans are the only creatures whose physical union is face-to-face. Now read Proverbs 5:18-19 and Song of Songs 4:9-11. What do we think these Bible passages say about sexual intimacy? How can these holy words shape our attitudes toward our own sexual lives?

The way the church communicates about sex does more harm than good. Billy Graham's old friend Malcolm Muggeridge said, "It must be admitted that we English have sex on the brain, which is a very unfortunate place to have it."

When people do not know what to say, they stay silent. Or in their ignorance, they say the wrong things. Christian people have been more embarrassed than appreciative of the human sexuality bestowed by their creator. If we teach that Jesus was a human being, then we must understand that he was a sexual being. We do not know exactly how he chose to express his sexuality. Throughout the ages the church as Jesus' body, has denied that Jesus was a vulnerable man with every temptation as any other man. And so, we accept that our Christ was effeminate, lifeless, weak, like some of the portraits of Jesus that hang in some of our homes and our churches.

Yet our culture talks and writes about sex every single day. And why would somebody struggling with sexuality want to come near a church that is known for anger, division, judgment, gossip, and arrogance? And so, they stay away. If the church communicates with compassion and sensibility, people can express themselves sexually in a place of acceptance and love.

Who are we sexually? What will become of us unless we understand our sexual selves? People fear pleasure or seek it with no constraints. In one of my books on joy, I quoted an attractive, accomplished single woman who said, "Love is a feeling. Sex is a sport."

Or as Madonna said, "Sick and perverted always appeals to me." And that attitude has been around for a long time. Mae West said, "Sex is an emotion in motion."

Using my gifts as a communicator, in my early years, it meant preaching. That expanded to teaching, writing, counseling, and radio and television. My life has expanded as I discovered the joy of the Lord in many opportunities that I never would have dreamed of, and that is incredibly humbling. With blessing comes responsibility to use our talents to fulfill the mission God is entrusting with us.

I discovered my gifts as a pastoral counselor with my studies in psychology of religion with Dr. John Davidson at Baylor University. Eventually, I became a licensed professional therapist with a doctor of psychology degree. And so, my calling to break the silence of the church on the sexual struggles of ordinary people came as I practiced psychotherapy with a host of places: private practice, Saint Joseph State Hospital, Family Guidance Center, Cedars Youth Services, Lutheran Family Services, Lincoln Regional Center, and Valley Hope Centers in Nebraska.

Most therapists soon find that clients are struggling with their sexual patterns. Sexuality is what people think it is. Some see it as shame, valued or worthless, a sport, art, beauty, evil or good, a source of freedom, a pleasure or a duty, a mysterious ecstasy, a skill, a sensory experience, a defense against loneliness, a form of communication, an aggressive tool to control, an ideal human state, a biological function, an escape, a reward, a way for rebellion, or a source of self-esteem.

Quality therapy can prevent the enormity of sexual despair now wrecking so many lives. Sexual feelings and healthy attitudes begin in our early life experiences. We need religious and spiritual leaders need to nurture appropriate sexual self-development.

The source of sexual anxiety relates intimately to the springs of all of life's difficulties. With sex, more than any other life transition, anxiety oozes out into our bodies. Silence must be replaced with compassion as people recognize suffering, even if we are blessed not to experience such afflictions.

I have found that life coaching skills with respectful questions that the client answers to be quite successful for those who have the skill to ask the right questions. The phrase psychotherapy comes from two Greek words: soul and healing. The early church and the New Testament are not silent about "healing the soul." Effective therapy frees people to become the best version of themselves.

Our current world and its culture did not discover sex. The sex revolution intended to frustrate, pain, and confuse those who took part. That's why I recommend pastors or denominational church leaders refer those struggling with life to seek out trained counselors. Only when God's children have a solid foundation of what their best self versions are like, can they become sexually fulfilled.

Families or congregations who are silent on sexuality often have much touchy-feely actions. They hug each other at any opportunity. Some wear seductive clothing. They offer a warm handshake as people come or go. Sexuality requires touching another person. It is quite healthy and spiritual. If humans are not touched, they do not live. Touching is needed all through the human life span. Baby girls have orgasms. Infant boys have erections. Contact between baby and parent is the foundation for later physical intimacy. Touching is the basis for all sexual relations.

Sexual excitement comes when people desire a feeling of being safely close, not stressed or pressured, cared for as we seek that early ecstasy again. Warm nurturing and nourishing by parents prepares us to become delightful lovers and dedicated parents.

Humans "fall in love" at various ages. Those who experience this love break their ties to childhood. It is a time to let go of parental security. So, to "fall in love" is to leave the physical image of our parents and turn to a new person.

People fall in love with the joy, but also with guilt, fear, anxiety, and anger, as they are experiencing helplessness. Sexual excitement is inspired by the rage to leave, to begin our own lives, to touch the new person. Passionate sex alone does not invoke our negative feelings.

Those who travel to do preaching or teaching or onsite writing can identify with the joy of returning home with passionate feelings. To the committed each separation gives a vision for pleasurable, comforting, and reassuring reunion through sex.

The kind of people who experience the most struggles with sex are those who are treated by professionals for personality disorders such as histrionics who secretly hide their emotional base while they stir up excitement for others.

Passive-aggressive clients are less obvious, but more numerous. If they are angered, they retaliate in secret fulfillment of their sexual needs. That is why one should never connect with a divorced person for two years following the separation,

Obsessive people tend to become extra-marital infatuated. They fantasize about others. To them, the present frustrations and pain need not exist in their realities.

Narcissistic and exhibitionistic being attached to only themselves, they do not care what others think. Most consciously do not realize what is happening. These are those who find someone needy in our churches. Soon that person becomes a new sex partner.

Some of our church members may have been taught that sexual ecstasy is somehow in line with religious sentiment. So, it becomes their habit to turn to heaven when one just cannot find a sustaining love on earth. Some would even say that that is what their belief and faith are all about.

This book does not answer the deeper questions about sexual pleasure. The answers are often complex than abbreviated generalizations. Those who live with depression or mood disorders and their effect on sexuality.

Only a professional therapist who majors on sexual therapy can offer the best resolutions to difficulties. The church cannot turn her head in silence. A psychotherapist can offer some directions than any aware human being may take for sexual fulfillment.

Proverbs is a scripture of wisdom that is male oriented, but can apply to either gender. With sex, the seductive person has the innocent human observing the nuances of fantasy, the time we are most vulnerable to sin. They come when our moods of fragile sadness when we are longing for some perfect union. Seduction can also come with rage or devastation following their seductive flattery, seeming concern, and attentiveness.

Once we are captured, our souls are in their hands. They continue to flirt and kiss and may now complain of our inner deadness. They will do anything for attention. They work hard for the love that they never received in their infancy. They then drop you and seek the love with their desperate tricks that they can never achieve.

All the communications about sex being a good thing and leading us to find the joys of a family who all love each other sounds so enlightening, but we all know that families are never perfect, especially church families. We are tainted by original sin. Often the best of us and the worst of us act in unloving ways. And that is the danger.

Sex creates a strong bond to enable us to stay true to our vows and commitment. Any therapist knows that sex contains an emotional element. Sex is not something that we just "do" with your body and leave your soul, your mind, and your brain. Sex has profound emotional consequences. As we examine the impact that the culture of his day and what it can tell us about the sexuality of Jesus. To discover the sexuality of the maturing Jesus, we attempt to look at Jesus as the women of the New Testament saw him. Most New Testament writers were male. So, the place of females in his life has never been given due consideration.

The foundation for the early Christian sexual life understanding was within the Jewish ethos. Quickly gentiles were in the majority, so the Greek views won out over the Hebrew understanding and practice.

There is no explicit comment in the New Testament regarding the way Jesus physically expressed his own sexuality. Scripture can give us some help, especially in such writings as the Song of Solomon, but we are left to be free and responsible to evaluate that aspect of his human journey in his 33 years on the earth.

Stifling the quest to know how to live sexually must come from a tender, compassionate heart. Being silent is never a healthy choice. A church of joy and love goes to the pinnacle and with the plunge of compassion, chooses to linger with us in our struggles when others move on. The Holy Spirit will cultivate within the church body the appropriate responses to life. And we will gather together as the tongue blesses, minds understand, and actions come from the mind of Christ.

Being a sexual self can be a journey to joy. Our intimate oneness grows deeper, better, more fun each year. Sex can give us a sacred place to escape from life and into the delight in the gift of each other. The intimacy we share, the exquisite pleasure we give, includes knowing a sheer joy. In Christ, we leave our hiding place of love as refreshed souls and bodies.

Humans have sexual lives so they can have children. Perhaps at one level of understanding, this does nothing to distinguish human sexual relations from animal sex. God created us to be sexual beings rather than beings who could create offspring by asexual means.

Sex is for the deepening of relationships. Sex brings personal intimacy. Some of the benefits of being sexual include unconditional acceptance, shared pleasure, and mutual comfort and affirmation. Sex is a sign that human beings are social creatures in need for companionship, friendships, and close relationships.

Let us start our spiritual struggle with a prayer. "Father God, thank you for giving us the gift of sexual intimacy so we can express our "one flesh" binding to bond in a physical way. We thank you loving God of joy for all the aspects of our physical intimacy that are good and mutually satisfying. Please help us to continue talking sensitively about our needs and how to happily fulfill them. Help us build a deeper and more pleasurable sexual relationship whatever season of life we are in. Enrich us in this spiritual struggle. We ask all this in the name of Jesus. Amen."

Hunter Thompson said it best, "Sex without love is as hollow and ridiculous as love without sex."

So next we turn to a discussion of love.

Chapter Two

What Do We Mean When We Say, "I Love You?"

No topic has captured people's attention and most every culture than the topic of love. All human beings are looking for love. At any age or time of life, we may be far from love but we never stop hoping the next opportunity is just over the horizon. Love is so frustrating. We are not ever able to just keep it. Like the sand slipping through our fingers, the harder and tighter we grasp it, the faster it falls away. All of us may remember our first love. Perhaps we experienced a delightful boy or girl who ignored us for somebody else. Love cannot be manufactured. It cannot be traded or bought. Love cannot be forced. No one can control love.

Life begins when each of us has a unique vision of love. Our uniqueness lies in our ability to conceptualize eternal joy. For most of us love is the most important thing in our lives. The first challenge of love is to unload the cultural baggage. Culture tells us that love is an object or state to be attained, fixed ideal.

Love requires us to reveal ourselves. C. S. Lewis, who taught at the University of Oxford, wrote, "To love at all is to be vulnerable. Love anything and your heart will be broken. If you want to make sure of keeping it intact, you must give it to no one." So much love pain comes with the vulnerability that comes with it. What do we mean when we say, "I love you?" We love having a fun time. We love football. We love food. We love music. A wonderful painting cannot reject us. Opening your heart to another person, even if you feel that you were seduced, is one of the most painful experiences in life. This kind of love experience is much worse than physical pain. It shakes us to the core of our identity, our hopes, our visions, or dreams. When we are "in love," we believe all the lies. We rush to a mountain-top, but when the fantasy love is lost, we are sent falling back to the unhappy valley below. We now feel completely empty. We think we are worthless.

We want our experience of love to be unconditional. Our media tell us that if we were just a little bit more attractive, a little thinner, and a little better dressed, then another person will take notice and we will be loved. The culture pressures us to set aside our reluctance and to give away our bodies. We think intimacy will lead to love. So, we just fantasize with watching movies and dreaming about it in novels. So that fake love experience is just a mirage and now we have nothing to show for it.

It is a spiritual struggle to look for love. To be loved, but not known is comforting but superficial. To be known and not loved is our greatest fear.

How can we open our hearts and know that in that moment, we will be accepted and not rejected? We do desire to keep the love show going. If we do admit the reality, we face the risk of being rejected, ridiculed, and thrown away. Only with the love of God and "the joy of the Lord," will we be filled with stability and confidence to face any rejection or loss. No matter how much earthly love hurts, your identity and value can never be shaken. And we will enjoy life and appreciate all the people and experiences that surround us every day.

Learning to live in the love of God is a process. We throw off the old nature and ways of thinking, and we have God's love in the loving Christ who lives within us, to direct us. Nothing we face during this brief earthly journey will shake loose the love of God.

There are at least four Greek words for love in New Testament writings. We hear the word love more than most other English word. We love our baseball team, our human lovers, oranges, steaks, babies, movies, fishing, or popcorn. Love is a verb, not a noun. Love is a living capacity within us that is present every day.

That fact that in English we have only one word for love leads to our never-ending confusion. Love as an addiction is considered an example of one with some personality disorder. Perhaps the woman who told me that "love is a feeling and sex is a sport" would fit that definition of love. Feeling to some means the love is real. "The love I feel for you" is an often-used phrase. However, feelings are variable. Today's passionate love may be regarded tomorrow as yesterday's infatuation.

Our society has assumed that the height of love is romantic love, an ecstasy and a torment. As children and youth, we use flower petals to reveal whether she or he loves us or not. People hope that love will rescue us. People insist that without the love of another, we're hopeless, insufficient, unable to live on our own. This thinking is what those high selling bodice-ripper novels offer. So, we are at the mercy of outside forces. In love at first everything is perfect. Then with some, everything is horrible. Lasting love exists from a lower voltage. Abundant life gives us endless opportunities to experience deep transformation, and lasting love. In concert with others, we are vulnerable to give and receive. We have our joy times, struggling times, sorrowful days, gains and losses. With real love, we find what it means to be part of something much bigger. Love involves courage.

In any marriage, there are occasions when spouses are highly angry with each other. We would not say they are out of love. They become back into the kingdom of love when they kiss and make up. Feelings are just too unstable to use as a criterion of love. No love connection is always easy or free of strife. How couples deal with conflict, their expectations, their commitments create an atmosphere for a sustainable relationship.

Loving couples allow dialogue. They see each other's perspective, and they move toward resolution. Thich Nhat Hanh, a native of Vietnam, always expands my spiritual space for love. He wrote, "The more you understand, the more you love; the more you love, the more you understand. They are two sides of one reality. The mind of love and the mind of understanding are the same."

There are at least three types of love. We talk about passionate love. What people often mean is that love involves intense arousal with a strong sexual base. French people use the word "jouissance" meaning exceeding joy or passionate joy. They use it for the times of unique sexual pleasure.

Romantic love is also used for passionate love. In literature, both are intense. Romantic love is different as it is focused on idealization of the other than chiefly the sexuality of the other. Both types of love occur early in a relationship. Romantic love is more of a fantasy that the other is perfect. Their qualities are often exaggerated with rapt attention to the experience of love to the exclusion of everything else. The romantic lovers desire to be together, but circumstances prevent it.

Companion love is the least intense type of love. This is what love becomes following a marriage. They have come to know each other well. Deep flames of passion have evaporated. If they love each other, passion can return. Afterward, the couple may then just drift into the business of living. As the local churches age, companionate love will be one factor in the silence of the church concerning sex. This does not mean couples are no longer "in love." Perhaps they now spend more time building more stable and permanent bonds and affection based on trust and common goals that replaces fantasy. The tendency to exaggerate the spouse's attributes is one characteristic of a happy marriage.

Now I am not saying that people who made sexual mistakes or bad choices cannot have a happy marital sex life.

A couple who wait until marriage learn about sex together. They learn from each other. They have no other to compare. They have no memories of other people to hinder their enjoyment of each other. It only causes pain when people possess the thought of being compared to another lover.

In a culture with a whole lot of sex going on, but not much love, I believe the church is the best way and the best place to share the details of a very real struggle that God's children face in trying to live real love in the world gone mad.

Saying I love you to a friend may just be a sexual attraction which is normal, but these relationships do not mean real love. Love means you want this person to be your partner for life. Love is when somebody to wake up with in the morning and who will lead you to heaven on earth now and in the future.

Love is not just a comfort or fun time when you are together. It would not be a good choice to get seriously involved or get married on that foundation alone.

Many congregations are full of spiritually struggling people who mistake lust for love. There is no such thing as one who is never tempted to sin. "The joy of the Lord is your strength." Pray daily. We are still running around in a human body, and your body remains programmed in certain human ways. When we leave our guard down and stop praying because we think we have all the answers we need, then we are in danger.

I continue to use my calling and gifts to enable us to experience joy, that authentic experience of love and joy that Jesus shared, the joy that comes from following Christ and living our lives according to God's instruction guide.

The positive emotion joy is part of the foundation for the higher realms of happiness. When our own cup is filled with joy, we will find it impossible not to share with others. Joy nurtures our sense of connection with the larger whole. We realize that the whole is only as healthy as its smallest part. Joy gives us an awareness of our inner abundance. In and because of joy we become more generous. We must be ministers of joy to the world. With joy, we notice our moments of happiness and the happiness of other people. The joy experiences that we share with others cannot be separated from our joy and happiness. Loving others is recognizing the human desire to live in joy and happiness. Simply breaking the silence about that is the foundation of love.

Paulo Coelho observed, "Anyone who is in love is making love the whole time, even when they're not. When two bodies meet, it is just the cup overflowing. They can stay together for hours, even days. They begin the dance one day and finish it the next, or such is the pleasure they experience, they may never finish it. No eleven minutes for them." If our desire is to live in the highest happiness, we must work to build a group of friends who accept and believe in being faithful in the sexual areas of your lives. This commitment will not be easy. We are not strong enough to do this by ourselves. We need a support group. If none of our un-churched friends will support us, then find a spiritual church youth group or for adults a gender group for men or women to find supportive friends. They should not be your only friends. Some of the best youth groups include scholars, athletes, cheerleaders, and those in leadership positions.

These are the ones who will anchor your soul to unshakeable joy. How could God "so love the world? "When we look at our world, we see people killing each other, making war, terrorist attacks, sexual distortion, sex trafficking, and horrible greed. With Christ inside, we can love everyone. Love is more courageous than all the terror in our world. If we do not break the silence, if we are not bold in our love, then hate wins. In an atmosphere that unveils love, joy and miracles happen. We look for the humanity and distortions behind the hatred. We realize our own pain is bound up with the pain of the world. Joy gives us the possibility of stretching ourselves, not in a coercive manner, where we judge ourselves as bad, but gently, with kindness and self-acceptance, we share our joy.

There is no better time than now to break the silence. Time is an implacable thief that steals away the gifts of life and the messengers of God who bestows them. As we grow older, we live with the knowledge that each day might be our last. It is normal not to believe it. As we share our joys and sorrows, we will discover moments of unimagined grace.

Chapter Three
Let Us Rejoice and Be Glad in It

When we break the silence, we rejoice and are glad that we have experienced passionate sex. In Christ's plan, we are aroused to know joy There is something new and exciting about our time on earth.

Oliver Wendell Holmes observed, "The human mind once stretched toe new idea, never goes back to its original dimensions." Once your soul has been opened to the highest happiness, everything about you will exude pure joy. Nobody reaches their highest potential. To rejoice and be glad comes when we believe we have reached our full potential by grace and guidance.

With gusto passionate people sing, "I've got peace like a river in my soul. I've got joy like a fountain in my soul." Life is like a river. Our silence may mean we are afraid of being swept away by the currents of the water. The culture of today causes people to stand on the banks of the river. Some enter the moving water and proceed against the flow. Some will stay on those safe banks. Some have never learned to swim. Those who can swim finish with disappointment on the journey. Those who jump in and go with the flow enjoy the feeling of being in the current. Their skills and talents enable those courageous souls to miss the rocks.

As a therapist and as a minister, I have observed what joy looks like in all of life and in sexual experiences. They do not resist happiness. They are in touch with all their senses, their images, thoughts, and feelings. They own a conscious and unconscious awareness that brings the gift of intense joy. They can transfer their insights from non-sexual moments to explicitly sexual times, whether they are alone or with some other person.

Many of my clients let pressures and concerns compete with appreciation of their beauty inside. Right thinking is the key to right living. What can we do to know the inner experience of self-knowledge that reflects the best version of our best selves including healthy, highly pleasurable sexuality.

It is sad that God's creation of sexual beings becomes a turbulent river With so much tension some see sex as a distortion by sin. Most sermons and books I read as a youth, thought that our sexuality drags us down into some evil path, chaining us to our sex urges, while our souls hunger for flying with God into freedom. So, in their silent thoughts, they see sex on earth as sinful lust.

If you use the Bible to help clients get healing insight, we could show them I Timothy 4:4, "For everything created by God is good, and nothing is to be rejected if it is received with thanksgiving."

How can we love what God has made and never talk about it? There are severe distortions concerning sex in the worlds of television, movies, books, internet, and cultural inventions. We must be sensitive to their agenda. Our society offers images that nobody can avoid. We are human beings. So sexual thoughts will pop into the mind uninvited. A person would have to hide in their basement to avoid all sexual images. Humans were created to respond to sexual stimuli. Nobody can control what pops into the brain. Martin Luther's words illustrate this human truth. He said, "You can't keep birds from flying around your head, but you can stop them from making a nest in your hair."

Once we make the choice to think about sexual acts and we enjoy the resulting arousal, we are in impure thoughts. A dieting person who spends time thinking about sundaes and doughnuts, one would want to eat it. Yummy food is hard to resist. The same dynamics go for sex. Temptation leads to undisciplined sex. These images hurt us. They have the power to do profound damage to real relationships, both now and in the future. The focus is on ourselves and our pleasure. This leads to utter selfishness and unrealistic expectations about sexuality.

Constantly worrying about our life decisions creates self-inflicted misery. Humans have a compulsion to compare and that results in jealousy, resentment, and anger. False impressions are the source of missing out on life. We read about picture-perfect marriages disintegrating.

James McReynolds

If we get to know somebody who "has it all," we observe the heavy crosses that they carry, envy dries up in a second. No one's life is anywhere near perfect. Every human being living on this earth takes shelter behind am asked to hide the uncomfortable truth that they are broken and in need of healing.

The acceptable solution is to offer our imperfect lives to God. Counting blessings each day will resurrect our joys. Allow God to fill you with awe. Pray Psalm 139:13-14, "You formed my inmost being; you knit me in my mother's womb. I praise you, because I am wonderfully made, wonderful are your works."

Let us rejoice and be glad that we can cling to God's timeless presence. Aging brings on a series of unpleasant surprises. Time is just wasted in getting plastic surgery and spending thousands of dollars on superficial beauty aids.

Eternal beauty is in our insides. It begins to show when our earthly beauty fades. There are few things more wonderful than to see two old people continuing to enjoy their sexual selves up until life itself ends. Being loving and caring is God's plan for us on our brief earth's journey as a happy harbinger of heaven to come.

When I review my life, I clearly recall times that appeared as a senseless struggle. However, God used it for his own purposes. As a young minister, I experienced what many naïve youths discover. There is a struggle and a realistic problem to be given a way in the current world of the ministry. Many of my moments of glory became oceans of failure and disappointment. I thought I had done everything possible in preparation, in prayer, and in honing my skills as I anticipated that one defining opportunity where I would my place in the kingdom work.

There have been many difficult adventures, but my blessings have outnumbered those difficulties, as my life is gradually being transformed by the Christ who dwells in me.

God directs my steps and fills each day with purpose. God turns ugliness into beauty, light from the darkness, and joy from pain.

Only his loving mercy will take my broken humanity and make something good out of all of it.

God has never wasted a moment of my life journey. Whenever I walk into a church building, a classroom, or an auditorium, or a radio or television studio, I feel at home. And when my heart senses that an audience is opening their minds and souls to my efforts to inspire and equip them with insights and living tools, I am overjoyed.

Healthy sexuality is more than positive thinking alone. The church that "dares greatly" will meet with resistance, but we must speak up. Consider the evil impact of distorted sexuality and pornography around the world.

Sex trafficking grows each day. This epidemic is now in indescribable tragic proportions, a costly obsession with degraded sexuality that continues to get worse with every passage of time. We see the signs in motels and hotels all over the world. At a Christian men's conference, the men and participating women were trained to spot and help victims of sex trafficking. These sex slaves are taken to commercial lodging places for sex. We must not stay silent. We must shake off our blinders and shake off the denial.

There are some clear signs that a person may be a sex-trafficking victim. They have few personal possessions. They act fearful and anxious in normal situations. They do not have their own identification nor do they have travel documents. They made look school age, but they are not in school. They will claim to be just visiting or passing through with no ability to clarify any reasons for their visit or their destination. They are not allowed to speak on their own behalf. Most of them are being deprived of water, sleep, medical care or food.

We live in a world where we must forever pick our way between delight in creation's gifts and the terrible sorrow for sin's distortions. We do rejoice in everything that God has given. We want to change and destroy the wrong uses of sexuality. Can we be clear of an action being a sinful, godless distortion or just something different or strange or unpleasant for most of us.

There is no distortion that cannot be swallowed up by the love of God. Impurity is everywhere in any large or small town, distracting us from what is of God and debasing of that which is beautiful and radiant.

When other humans are objectified makes us self-centered. As objects to be used for self-gratification sinful distortion diminishes any compassion or empathy for others. The more we grow in compassion and love, the closer we draw to Divine Love.

As creators and guardians of culture, informed and committed people are now in a perfect position to help turn the tide from obscenity and back to how God wants us to think and act in our minds, hearts, and souls.

God desires standards that are high and his Word God encourages us to do the same. We must create an atmosphere in every congregation that fights for his will. We must not continue in despair at our own sin, but we must fight for wholesome values, and we pray for the grace to persevere in holiness in our private lives.

All of us has sinned and come short of the glory of God. Maybe we need fine-tuning of how we show ourselves in speech, body language, dress, and thoughts. The whole lifespan is needed for growing into the person God created us to be. Each step we take toward God's love leads us to heaven. We must stay humble and curious about the ways of God, which are not our ways, but in our searching, we soak up more grace. Each phase of our journey prepares us for the next, as God builds his kingdom, brick by brick, through our simple acts of love.

In the heavenly kingdom, we will be capable of unbounded intimacy. And if sexuality is good, then in heaven, all of creation will never be destroyed but it shall be enhanced. If sexuality is new and different in heaven, it will be because it will be more, not less exciting than it was on earth.

By our depersonalization of our sex actions we dehumanize people. Humans are being sexual in the quiet hours of communication and contemplation as much as in the volcanic moments.

The current cultural exploitation of sex shrink sexuality, because it concentrates on orgasm and things that stimulate bodies. Our message must teach us that sexual fulfillment is achieved when a personal relationship sustains a human sexual relationship. We are wholly beautiful.

We will shout our reverence for each other. We are called the temples of the Holy Spirit. This metaphor points to a unity, a spiritual connection of a meaningful body and an eternal soul. Someday in Christ we shall be cleansed, glorified, and transformed into the best version of ourselves for all eternity.

One reason the church has been so silent about sexuality and spirituality is that so little was known about sexuality. We now know more about integration of the sexual with other aspects of the self. The concern is to preserve an appreciation for the beauty and value of sex and to explain how sexuality and spirituality complement each other.

God's love is passionate. So, God is sexual. So, the integration of sexuality and spirituality means to love God properly and to not to emphasize the importance of the physical act of sex. To integrate sexuality and spirituality is to appreciate the goodness, to cherish the richness it brings to life. It is also to exercise one's sexuality with the will of God.

Sexual intimacy is enhanced with a healthy spirituality. This intimacy is improved when partners have the spiritual strength to risk rejection of each one's new ideas for variety and managing the anxiety of self-disclosure.

We can and do rejoice in gladness because of sexuality. In heaven, we will know the highest happiness. We will be much more, not less, sexual in the image of God in heaven. All earthly perversions of sexuality are overcome, especially selfishness. When all egotistic perversions are eliminated, all pleasure is increased, including sexual pleasure. In heaven, we will rejoice and be glad in it.

Even if sex was not "spiritual," there would be sex in heaven because of the resurrection of the body. The body is not a mistake to be remade. The body is not a prison cell to be freed from, but a divine work designed to show forth the soul as the soul shows forth God in glory.

Our spiritual intercourse with God is the ecstasy merely hinted at in all earthly intercourse, physical or spiritual. The ultimate reason to rejoice and be glad is that sexual passion is so strong, so different from our other passions.

That mystery is beyond our grasp. We tremble to stand outside ourselves in the other, to give our whole selves, body and soul, because we are made in the images of God the sexual being. We love the other sex because God loves God.

Living in the fire of love is our destiny in God's intention when the earthly journey is completed. Earthly sex is only a shadow. We are rejoicing in the process of thickening ourselves so that we will become that heavenly fire.

Chapter Four

It's Time to Have the Talk with the Church

Church has tremendous power in our culture. Our songs are about sex. And we publish books and magazines that have the agenda of offering tips on how to enjoy sex, the freedom of the sexual revolution to enjoy the pleasures of sex with just anyone.

Magazines sold in the grocery store allure us in. And those at the truck stop are even more graphic. Statistics show that most women and men think about sex every day.

The Bibles we teach and preach from has much more material about sex than the culture thinks. The Song of Solomon paints an eye-opening picture of what redeemed sex looks like. The sexual imagery in this scripture is written in surprising detail. Those in the church say they read the whole Bible every year. If they read the Song of Solomon, they will never think about wells, trees, cisterns, and fruit the same way again.

Our sexuality is a divine creation. God designed it. Campus ministries At the University of Nebraska and Southeast Community College in Lincoln took a survey of incoming freshmen and asked them, "How much influence did your church play in the development of your views of sexuality? Less than two percent said that their church had something to do with their views on sexuality.

A few wrote in personal comments. One said, "People in my church do not believe in sex." Another wrote, "Our church is boring. They never talk about sex or dating or what marriage means. It's just as well. They would make that boring also." Still another said, "In our youth group, we talked a little bit about sex but avoided any of the juicy stuff."

For 20 years I served as volunteer campus minister in Lincoln, every year a brand-new crop of freshmen entered the "college experience" each year. I have been blessed to "have the talk" with hundreds of them.

Most have never turned to the biblical view, including professors and even ministers in the church. Too long the church's "talk" has not centered on sex as a gift from God. Any biblical view rides on the fine line between the errors of having sex whenever we desire it and legalistic talks about sex being for procreation only.

Church people today have not a shred of awareness that their people as so infatuated with sex. One reason is that the human body is the height of God's creation during our journey here on earth, now and beyond.

We desperately need the talk because sex, the powerful mingling of two souls and bodies, is the most sought-after experience.

"The talk" should tell people that there is nothing healthy about casual sex. Medical practitioners including nurses, physicians, sex therapy experts, or scientists will tell you there is a sexual revolution and that the aim of life is to enjoy dynamic passionate sex. It is not a surprise that people choose to be casual about sexuality. We must tell the church that sex unites the souls and bodies of two people. And that is never casual.

God created sex to give enjoyment for a husband and wife. Sex was for the mutual pleasure of both. "The talk" must bring silence to the thought that Satan created pleasure. God does not create evil. The pleasure we receive when we eat delicious food, or smell a rose, or make love is from God.

Dancing with God and each other with the sound of music elicits great pleasure. A wedding worship service gives place to "the talk" that couples need to continue to be romantic, and to enjoy each other spiritually, emotionally, and physically.

One thing will be approved by everyone. We can talk about God's gift of sex so that we could produce children. The first command from God was to "be fruitful and multiply and replenish the earth. We have been quite faithful to that command and it shows.

The church does not have to be persuaded to have children, but sadly, there is no sexual enjoyment in their lives. They experience no unity or intimacy. Sexual intimacy involves more than just having children.

Why do we think that Saint Paul had to give "the talk" in the early churches? Sexual immorality was rampant in the culture. Many new Christian men had several wives. Temple prostitution was a form of worship to the false gods. Women in Paul's day were honored to serve as a temple prostitute. Men and women used their slaves for sexual gratification.

Quite a few of the early converts to Jesus were Gentiles. So, Paul saw the need to teach them what is right and wrong about sexual purity. The Gentiles had grown up in a culture where anything was acceptable. People found pleasure in any way they wanted it. That culture was not so different from the culture where we live now.

The Sex Revolution has crossed all boundaries. In the right context people do have different kinds of sex that can be so unbelievably intense. Individuals experience times of a deep joy experience beyond anything expected.

Coupled with deep love transcend the physical. Everything is involved including the mind, body, the spiritual being. Some report that they saw God. I asked, "What did God look like? "God came with an amazing white and purple light," he said. This light was soft, sort of like a cloud." It felt like not being physically there, just floating along in that safe, bright, peaceful, joyful light. These ordinary people experience something new that our parents and grandparents never knew." Beyond just normal orgasm, it was a spiritual connection so deep I just could never describe." Time passed quickly.

This is the way it is supposed to be. Highest human happiness includes seeing fireworks and hearing angels sing.

Nobody can get that surprising joy every time. The spiritual and sexual selves are not separated. Some couples pray before sex. Communion with God brings a sense of wholeness and peace.

Those who are graced this way, being free in Christ and bringing nonhappy baggage, couples transcend self-consciousness and self-judgment. "The talk" might be a part of an adult group retreat including people from30 to 90 years of age. The church is silent about sex among the older people. It is possible for humans to have sex until the day they die.

Tragically most people know only low pleasured sex. Some would say that their sex satisfies them. However, some find that highest pleasure and beyond. Few could ever be taught how to do or want that. Age is not a factor. Couples focus on specific sensations and allow sexual pleasure to take them to another dimension beyond ordinary pleasure. There is no word to describe the ineffable joy. I think the French word *jouissance* lights my fire.

Few people, especially Christians, are talented as sexual athletes in the bed room. The potential to deepen sexual joy is limitless. All life changes from dull black and white to vivid colors in the crackling flame of a wood fire, the smell of clean sheets, words from a romantic book or poem, powerful music that lifts them right up into the air or as if they ride music like a roller coaster. Smells are delightful.

They feel the capacity to be fully alive. Sex never gets dull. Enjoying Sex with same partner year after year brings joyful repeats, because when one touches or is touched by the lover, they feel as if they are making love for the first time.

How can our awesome God be so narrow as to create the best spiritual and physical sexuality for those committed in marriage? God is love. And God is sexy.

The research literature reports more people in the upper socio-economic income brackets have had more pre-marital intercourse and extra-marital sex and those in lower income brackets. More than 80 percent of church members including pastors report having had pre-marital sex. Even though the majority experiences pre-marital sex, the leadership of churches believe and teach that sexual expression of sex is reserved only for marriage.

So, churches continue to be silent even with the horrid human problems caused by abuse of sex in society.

There is so much pressure to have sex in the college years. Students tell us that they do not think it's possible to find a person who won't breakup with them in college if you don't have sex. They assume all college relationships involve sex.

There is unbelievable pressure to have sex in college. Your son and daughter are now on their own. They see themselves as adults for the first time. So, they want to do what adults do. They do not just have girlfriends and boyfriends. Adults have affairs have affairs.

College students living in dorms with males and females have ways to keep each other out of the room while they are having sex. Campus health centers pass out contraceptives as if they are giving out candy bars.

So, the "talk" with college students involves their learning how to be careful as they go off to college. We must change the minds that suck them into madness that is all around them.

The church must teach that every college relationship does not involve sex. None of mine did. I did attend a Baptist college where sex was not near as prevalent as in huge universities. I speak at colleges all over the world, and I constantly meet wonderful, smart, impressive students who understand and live a life of chastity.

"The talk" that breaks the silence must include the reality that our sexual yearnings are a yearning for God, our eternal lover. So, sex can then be a sacrament. In my Protestant tradition, baptism and the Holy Communion or the Lord's Supper are the sacraments practiced. Whenever two people are sexually intimate with one another, that is a holy moment. Some people in our culture today reduce sexuality to just "doing it" or "putting a little excitement into life" or "dealing with loneliness for the night."

Those without Christ influencing their daily decisions cannot in the most remote way see sexual times as holy. They cannot imagine that people are getting their hands onto another person's soul when they have sex with them. That's the reason people carry so much hurt, misery, and guilt from their sexual experiences out of marriage. Their souls will never be the same again unless forgiveness, change, and redemption come into save them from all the pain.

There is so much confusion about sex. People have used it and misused it. God's love gift has been perverted and exploited. Breaking God's boundaries leads to death and utter unhappiness.

This "talk" must be presented with compassion and healing to those who have acted outside the will of God. Churches join the Kingdom Joy movement with sweet forgiveness. Only then can they know and feel in their hearts that they have been forgiven. Help them to know that they are not "damaged goods."

The grace and good news of the gospel is for the whole person. It is good news to us as we make our befuddled attempts to live with our sexual selves. Our relationship to Jesus Christ cannot mean salvation from sexuality, as some churches teach. It does not mean some new rules or more boundaries. The Word of the Lord is one of grace and freedom. Grace is not about being against nature or any of God's gifts, but it tells us about distorted nature. Grace never puts sex down. Grace liberates sexuality as a power for love. Becoming a Christian does not mean a suppression of sexuality. The "talk" offers some insight into the positive role of sex for abundant living. I am writing about the new spiritual environment for joyful sexuality.

This has been my vision for the church "to create an atmosphere where joy and miracles happen."

Too often people are dissatisfied with some aspects of sex. So, they blame each other for being flawed in some way. The root of the problem lies with the acceptance of the culture's messages about the way sex should and ought to be. Sex therapists change huge amounts to focus on something instead of changing one's self. Their goal is genitally focus orgasm as the goal.

The Silence of the Church

This is not a book about the effects of the Sex Revolution, but it is to break the silence so that we can enable people to find the highest happiness and some joy.

Salvation can mean that people can empower themselves. Christ living inside of us enables us to rejoice when we do things right so that we can take advantage of the potential for sexual joy.

To not having any conversations about sexuality and its abuses is spiritual abuse. Spiritual abuse is when a congregation or a denomination repeatedly insists than have the truth, and if you go anywhere else, you will miss out on God's will or even heaven.

Spiritual abuse eventually shows up when pastors use ministry to gain power and wealth as they manipulate and lie to earn more money. They use exclusive language. They say, "We are the only ones who respect and interpret the Bible correctly. We are New Testament Christians with the only correct theology. Everyone else is wrong, misguided, and ignorant."

They cultivate a dependence on one leader for all information about any part of life including sexuality.

They demand allegiance. It becomes their way or no way. These people create an atmosphere of fear and shame, centering on what they think about sexuality. There is absolutely no grace for someone who fails to live up to the church's expectations. And if someone steps outside the silence or the unspoken rules, leaders shame them into compliance. Those who force young women who get pregnant out of wedlock to confess their sin in public worship is sexual and spiritual abuse. They usually do not force a young man to do the same.

The continuing spiritual sex revolution is one aspect of authenticity and joy. The silent churches are not willing to navigate sad and chaotic times and to connect with God, so they are not enabled to love and to be compassionate. The silence is encouraged with their alliance with the powerful political reality. For that and other reasons, people declare, "We refuse to buy it." Millions are going away from the church. They refuse to worship the Caesars of today.

I was introduced to Julian of Norwich at the University of Oxford. She lived in the fourteenth century in England. Julian was a spiritual woman who lived out her devotion and security in God. She wrote and taught that everything in life, even terrible events or bad choices would ultimately turnout in God's ultimate will. Her theology is summed up in her words, "All shall be well, and all manner of things shall be well."

All my life I have been reluctant to claim the immense joy and happiness found in God's gift of sexuality. I had the sense to know that I would be subjected to ridicule by some of my fellow Christians, especially those who are my peers. This among other excuses kept me in silence about being so public and permanent despite Jesus' invitation to live a life of love.

Those who joined me in this pursuit of happiness have been my guides on exploring the exciting sexual frontiers not ever well defined or understood. Through each voice, each memory of joy, and the clear images, I have been blessed to share with others.

Those who break the silence are spiritual pioneers who have pushed the boundaries of conventional sexual response. Those who are "daring greatly," as Theodore Roosevelt said in a speech on "Citizenship in a Republic" in 1910 in Paris, challenged us to view a connection of body, mind, emotion and spirit, that is the ultimate connection tithe meaning of life.

God would support our description of an experience of passion that is so profound that it defies attempts to package it or to attach a precise formula to it. Each person's journey is unique and is new territory for those who think there is a well-worn and familiar path to enjoying the abundant life. The challenge is to break new ground and to explore endless possibilities. This gift is still lying dormant, lost for years like a buried treasure, but waiting to be unearthed. This hidden treasure can be recovered, brought to the surface, where the gift will be enjoyed because it belongs to those who know the mystery of God's creation.

Chapter Five

How Did I Get to Be 75 When I Feel Like 25?

Sexuality simply does not exist for our invincible older adults. The church remains silent about older people. Our culture says that old people are asexual and the consensus is that physical attractiveness depends on youth and beauty. Those under 30 and the youth have difficulty believing that older people are sexual beings. This false assumption would mean acceptance of parents as having sexual interest.

In most congregations, today most of the members average out to be about 60 years of age. They are a silent majority. The culture and the church acts like people past 70 have no sexuality. Our culture pictures sexuality among older adults is funny. Many birthday cards for seniors deal with sex in later life as a humorous joke. Comical cards to those of old age contain words about physical weakness and failures in sexual performance.

Age does not have to bring inactivity or immobility. Humans can have until the day they die. Overt sexuality in older ages is far more likely to be denied to older women than older men.

How can the church teach older adults how to relate to pleasures that connect to ecstasy? Of course, they build on what they already know. Loving souls of all ages can help seniors open to new ways of feeling, sensing, thinking, and imagining the possibilities. They can then fully transfer their joys to their sacred gift of sexuality. In Christ, they are free to reflect on any life experience that brings them pleasure. Have them consider what they enjoy and love about those experiences. What was involved as they take responsibility for that sheer joy. What did they do or let go of to have such a joy?

A group of kindred souls can use their own words or metaphors or images to describe the joy as clearly as possible. How did you deepen your enjoyment throughout this experience? Help them feel aware of the human senses such as taste, sights, hearings, or smells. This awareness is critical for intensifying meaningful pleasures.

Transfer their new awakenings to their enjoyment of this pleasure to their gift of sexuality. Spiritually and mindfully, we can take the next step. Jesus promises us abundant life, but not perfect synchronicity but to simply allow feelings and choices to arrive inside as if they are dancing with God. God gave us natural rhythms in our bodies that cause aware of all the senses involved. Some have reported a "sixth" sense reserved for the moments of

passionate sex. How do mature older people say about sex as beyond pleasure? They speak of something beyond human concepts. They speak words such as passion, peace, joy, and wholeness. This loving gift brings limitless possibilities. It brings connection to God and the universe. And this is what breaking that silence can accomplish.

A silver-haired man is admired for his voracious sexual appetite in old age. Men with power and money have an aphrodisiac that goes on until they die. Culture insists that older women seeking sex are ridiculous. She is to stand back and not get emotionally involved. Intercourse may not be part of an older woman's sexual energy. She can still have deep and intimate friendships. Warm and radiant, she is given the trust to enter feelings of another human being when barriers that separate are dissolved and she meets another face to face, and her creative work requires her sexual energy. And so, her sexual energy with deep emotion and inner power flows into affirmation of life instead of denying her gift of abundant life.

Our culture usually discards older women. As women become older, they can shed dependency and are given the gift of a clearer picture of themselves and the meaning of their lives. So, she can express her vitality in new, uninhibited ways and with deeper satisfaction.

Our talk to the silent church helps mature women see themselves as God sees them. Older women and older men are increasing in beauty through all the ages of life. Prayerful, joy-filled women become more beautiful as they age, not less.

As a woman matures spiritually, growing wisdom and holiness, she reflects a radiant inner beauty that touches others in countless ways. She brings joy and miracles to the world. The church cannot afford to put away older people, but must increase ministries by and for them. The "talk" must redefine the cultural perception of aging. Faith and true beauty go hand in hand. Proverbs 30:31 reveals that "a woman who fears the Lord is to be praised." Women can learn this best from other Christian women.

The church must wake up from their silent perspective and invite people of all ages to come out of the cold of the youth-obsessed culture.

Our bodies will separate from our souls at our time of death. With the power of the resurrection of Christ, the bodies of the faithful will be raised and glorified, reunited with our souls, incorruptible for all eternity. In reading the book of Genesis, we learn that human beings were happy, innocent, and naked. A detail pointed out that nakedness was often linked with human shame. Nakedness started out as a joy, not an embarrassment. Adam and Eve were made for each other, real soul mates not meant to be alone. They reflected God's "very good" creation. It is sin, missing the mark, that has caused our human bodies to suffer the consequences including, aging, pain, and sickness.

People with whom God began a good work with our active passionate sexual lives in younger days are more likely to continue active in their older days.

For most people, sexual activity does decline with advancing years. The decline is medical or psycho-social, and time related. As we age, there Isa delay in arousal, with need of genital stimulation. The penis becomes more rigid, and we need vaginal lubrication.

Medical causes include drugs that cause impotence or lack of desire. Diseases also lead to impotence. Surgery of the prostate or uterus, catheters, poor mobility, change in body image, or amputation and depression lead to a loss of interest in sex.

The psych-social factors include having no partner, a lack of privacy in nursing or retirement homes, and social conditioning lower chances for the joy times when we had such tremendously miracle sex.

Some important insights include the fact that sexuality remains important throughout a person's life. Maintaining sexuality in its many forms should be encouraged to promote health, faith, hope and love in older adults. Also, an open and receptive attitude by ministers, lay persons, and professional therapists should encourage older adults to discuss their sexual problems. Keep in mind that many sexual problems in older adults can be addressed in a similar manner to those for youth and younger people.

Until the end of life we have more experiences of feeling overwhelming love or a spiritual time surrounded by beauty and peace. During the time we feel so loved, but some dismiss it because it is not rational. Something like this may happen while you are enjoying morning sunrise. We cannot find words to describe it. John Wesley, the founder of the Methodist faith, put his experience in words later saying, "I felt my heart strangely warmed."

The body is not an effective differentiator of what is going on inside our souls. I recall with joy the day Dr. Norman Vincent Peale anointed me as minister of joy to the world. I felt so excited and enthusiastic that I felt physically ill. I was aware of being loved by God, other people, and myself. It was the same experience I had in the Vanderbilt University Benton Chapel that I was making myself available to God for a call to share the joy of the Lord with the world.

Many older adults trip on fumbling wordings. Their bodies sometimes rejoice with intense sexual feelings as the deepest parts of soul and body together are aroused. They report that they feel so out of control as they reconcile these intense feelings of being with God with sexual feelings. Slowly grandma or grandpa relaxes and is at peace.

Most of these mystical experiences bring joy. Life's purpose and your personal calling and the insight that you have been chosen to do ministry that transforms not only you but that which brings joy to the whole world. A lifetime of prayerful companionship with God brings comfort to all creation in ways you will never know until you see the glass of God not dimly, but clearly and completely.

There will be more older adults on this earth than any other age. The church must not be silent about putting them out of sight, out of use, when they still have the most to give.

Where you are now living and what kind of body shape you are in, you will always have something to share. You are so needed to fulfill the call to give the eternal energy of love into the vast universe.

Christ resides inside of you. You can have continual awareness of God within for transforming our consciousness. This gift is the most powerful gift that God gives you. During the Holy Communion or our Lord's Supper, brings physical and emotional comfort. Our mothers fed us through her own body. Being fed established a nurturing, intimate connection to love that our subconscious memories we associate with food and the act of eating and drinking until the end of our lives.

Sexual imagery is found in the Bible and in the writings of mystics to symbolize the union of God with the soul. A person can live a long and happy life without a physical sexual event. However, none of us could live without feed and drink.

Spiritual food as we eat and drink in Holy Communion assures us that we are being loved and nurtured. Jesus initiated this sacrament to be our love symbol of himself because he knew that the love connection between food and love was so natural. Lovers think about their loves every minute they are awake.

Jesus created a new reality for encouragement and times of vital remembering of the love connection. Even the church is so filled with self-righteous attitudes and the blindness of greed that they must isolate and become unaware of God's creation. Our Lord combined the spiritual with the material by choosing bread and wine for representing himself. This holy food is available to the poorest of us. It is not just food for the wealthy, but for those who are the children of God.

An older member of one of my congregations had a communion experience during our open food bank. The warm loaves of bread offered had been baked from the same ingredients. Other folks would say, "That sure looks good." He offered them the opportunity to break off a piece. He shared that this experience was one of intimate communion for him.

During spiritual gatherings, I ask the participants if they would like to live to be 120 years old. I share my own history of preaching my first sermon at age 12. I have said that I would like to live 112 years, so I can serve my God's calling to preach for 100 years. As far as I know, no preacher has lived and preached that long. One Virginia Baptist preacher was said to have preached for a century and died at age 118. This is thought to be an old Appalachian folk story.

Most people say they would not want to live that long. They sometimes reason that all their friends would be dead. So those extra years would not add one day of higher happiness.

Saint Paul gave some insight into this mystery when he wrote: "It makes me happy to suffer for you, as I am suffering now, and in my own body to do what I can to make up all that has still to be undergone by Christ for the sake of his body, the church. I became a servant of the church when God made me responsible for delivering God's message to you."

For the new Joy Movement, every congregation will grow spiritually with the development of small groups of older adults, no more than eight or ten, who gather intentionally to share their faith. These groups enrich the lives of those desiring support and encouragement.

The groups could meet in homes for prayer, sharing, and a small meal. Some older, active retired minister would be the best spiritual guide for the group. Members of this special spiritual group would be committed to spiritual growth of one another until the day they die.

We called an older grouping our church the Invincible Ones. This gathering demonstrated to our church and community that love does overcome the fear of loneliness, deprivation, and the disabilities of old age. All this is accomplished within the shadow of the church steeple.

My ministry in the lovely Blue Ridge Mountains with six United Methodist congregations was called the Max Meadows Circuit. Each church was approximately six miles from each other. All were affiliated with the Methodist denomination, but each was different as night and day.

It was a happy time for a unique ministry. When I was appointed there, one of the leaders of the Brick Church, frankly said, "We told them not to send no educated preacher up here." I told them that there were so many things I did not know. They taught me so many things such as how to shoot guns, how to hunt and fish, how to exist with the energy coming from "the joy of the Lord as my strength."

There was much competition between each church, even in the apple butter making, which gave them much of their budget. Turning over their tithes and offerings to the church was not always their style. Someone had embezzled thousands of dollars in past years, so there was a lack of trust. I'll just summarize my time there by saying it was a difficult experience, and I used every gift and grace that God had blessed me with. Even though I was the appointed pastor, I was not invited to do a wedding or funeral for the first six months.

Next door to the parsonage lived a gifted Presbyterian pastor. We enjoyed a deep spiritual bond. The Presbyterians had a long history of building churches in the Blue Ridge Mountains. After graduation from seminary, a pioneering missionary minded man, built wonderful congregation that were built with river rock, and stand today as a monument for selfless faith. Vaughn Earl Hartselle, my Presbyterian colleague, shared his own ways of serving the churches. His insight and experience helped me to bring the joy of Christ to a people who had been fed with a traditional, unhappy, and unbending spiritual life.

Vaughn Earl shared a story of the church planting work of Presbyterians. He noted that when they first visited people in the mountains about organizing a Presbyterian church, they would ask, "Are there any Presbyterians around here?" One reply was, "Well, there are some possum, lots of deer, and a bear or two, but I don't think we have any Presbyterians around these parts."

I attempted to treat each congregation with equal love and care. I was quite proud of them and after the first year, each church received gold medal designation from the Holston Conference for evangelism. We had huge Vacation Bible Schools. As a young man in my prime, I played games with the children, volleyball and basketball with youth and young adults.

People of all ages told me that saw the joy of Christ in me. I could use my counseling skills as every human problem imaginable came up.

There were many older adults in every church. Hospital calls took me to Charlottesville, Durham, and Winston-Salem. One of them was a man named Bill Moore. He looked like Babe Ruth and had been a legendary baseball player for a community team. He still had several of the baseballs that he had hit for long distances.

His son had cancer and Bill rode with me on my visits to minister to him and his family. In his son's last days, I spent hours with him watching John Wayne shows and old western movies.

After his son died, Bill would invite me to roam the hills, ford the creeks, and to go fishing. On one occasion, we caught beautiful rainbow trout adnate them for supper. The first time I tossed the lure out toward the water, my line got struck in a tree. Bill laughed and said, "Now, Dr. Jim, they aren't no fish in them trees."

Bill told me that I was the only preacher who ever would watch a NASCAR race with him. He enjoyed baseball. We watched the

College World Series in Omaha on television. Together we picked LSU as our favorite, and they won the national championship with a walk off home run.

People become quite vulnerable as they establish deep trust with the love that helps them to reveal their very souls. One day after supper, Bill and I had talked outside in the summer breeze. Bill reflected, "Pastor, in my old age, I don't get as good an erection I used to. I guess it's just my age."

He then was quite vulnerable as he asked, "Do you really think that any of us old folks are sexually attractive? Only some crazy person would want to do anything with us?"

I assured him that people of older years are indeed sexually attractive. Think about all those around you. Look at the hands, the eyes, and the wrinkles that are symbols of living, loving, and hurting. Those lines across your face are love lines. Feel the warmth of your wife and those who are close to you. See how you feel when you smile at each other. Older people do not need to fall for that same discrimination that others cast upon you. If older people do not teach us the beauty of aging, who will? There are benefits of aging as it relates to sexuality. Relate to people for what they are, how they are, and how they have been, not just how they look right now. Don't tell me that some of your mountain men have not already looked around and seen some people you would not mind laying a bear hug on.

Our last years of life bring changes in our hair, our eyes, our ears. Memory, intelligence, mobility, high blood pressure, circulation changes are affected by the oldest principles. Use it or lose it is correct for the process of aging, and that is certainly true for human sex. Brain chemistry also changes our sexual activity. Our culture must advocate that sexuality is vital in our aging years and is expected in our aging populations. Continuing to be sexual later in life is a huge factor in longevity.

Breaking the silence is the new challenge for a new sex for our current time. What a new and joy-filled progress could be taught in the home, school, and church, if we find an enduring, committed, comfortable intimacy that goes beyond the limits of the body to the potential of the merging of two spirits.

Chapter Six

The Silence and the Shame of Sexual Violence in the Church

What a sense of silence and shame does to those who have suffered from sexual slavery, rape and sexual violence cannot be fully realized.

Churches and especially many clergy, are under the impression that Sexual violence is not an essential issue facing the church. The response of the church in situations of sexual abuse really does matter. This book is intended to bring light to an issue that is cloaked in darkness. The church could give a voice to victims silenced by the church and society to understand the prevalence of sexual abuse. Many pastors tend to be naïve when it comes to the probability that both victims and offenders exist within the church. Where is God in all of this? Sexual violence is a sign of power abuse. Countless courageous women who have broken the silence on sexual violence have given credence to the fact that the Church is not immune to the sin and crime of violence.

We go to church expecting a caring, nurturing environment, a safe place to grow in faith. Women and children are especially vulnerable to sexual assault and exploitation. Secrets are kept. Rumors are spread. People take sides and often against the side of the victim.

Many offenders are husbands, fathers, brothers, sisters, ministers, priests, husbands, grandfathers, and leaders of church-sponsored groups. Church is no longer a safe place. Members quit the church. Any sexual violence is spiritually destructive. If a blanket of silence exists, then violence breeds and our innate capacity to create some course of action is paralyzed.

Several years ago, a conservative fundamentalist woman was strongly in joyful anticipation as she entered a state university. One of the first actions on campus was to join the campus ministry. What she found in this group completely surprised her. When she told her parents how uncomfortable she felt, they just affirmed the misguided, harmful, and shame giving exclusive ideas that she had found in her church. She recalled that this group was misogynistic. They tried to paint a picture of sexual energy filled with judgment. They insisted that God was this hyper-masculine being who was physically a man. She soon after left her traditional family's faith.

She did meet another young woman who helped her in her struggle to reconcile this image of God. None of her past friends would have anything to do with her. The sexual abuse and date rape violence cut her soul into two parts.

She finally decided to join the women's movement which became her new church. Women were suffering not just from their search for equality and justice. She observed horrific sexual violence. The culture of accepted rape and violence caused her to suffer skepticism and blame from the victim-shaming people everywhere she turned.

Nothing has really changed from past experiences of powerful and physically strong males who are exempt from the rules. Unfortunately, stories of abuse and sexual violence even on the Christian campus are rampant.

Sexual assault is any oral, vaginal, or anal penetration that is forced upon another. Women are usually the victims. And men are the perpetrators. Women rape victims are three times as likely among college women than the general population according to seminars on the subject by experts. The effects of a sexual assault are not only physical, but mental and psychological problems such as post-traumatic stress disorder and chronic depression. According to the University of Nebraska in Lincoln, many drop out of school after an assault. Prevention of sexual assault needs to be a first priority on the college campus.

Young people are not being taught, or are being taught ineffectively, basic information on sex and sexuality. The myths of rape acceptance in social norms bring false information. No information causes attitudes toward sexual activity including debut and alcohol use and eventual completed rapes. Investigation of the level of acceptance of rape myth in college students would help in developing tools for prevention intervention.

Fraternities sometimes encourage violence against women. Their norms and practices including loyalty, secrecy, and group protection and heavy use of alcohol creates an atmosphere conducive to rape. So, if fraternity men are encouraged to engage in sexually violent acts which are supported by their peers and institutional norms, women, with whom they have considerable social contact are at a high risk for sexual assault. The risk of sexual assault among sorority women is likely to be greater than the general female population. Most of the victims knew their attackers, as do women who are not in college. Most sorority women do not report rapes. So, with an environment of silence, some think of rape of women is "safe."

Our churches continue to remain silent. The congregations that are supposed to serve as society's moral heartbeat and compass for living is hopelessly irrelevant. More than three-fourths of women surveyed who have experienced sexual violence are church regulars.

Gender equality is now in the workplace where more and more women are serving in high level positions. So, the tables are turned so that the least instance of male harassment gets the male fired. Our culture and the church stands apart as a largely closed system to reform. This foundation comes from poor interpretations of the Bible that feeds an undercurrent of pre-marital purity and abstinence. Any "talk" about sexual violence among church people is rare. They still believe violence occurs somewhere else. The huge swampland of sexual violence, rape, abuse, disrespect, and the behaviors that lead there, remain the darkest, most shameful shame on the church. There is a deep ignorance and misunderstanding of women's bodies and a tone deafness to the trauma of rape. A powerful politician often says, "The women have ways to just shut down that whole thing."

The prudish, patriarchal culture persists from the numerous abuse scandals In the Catholic church. The media focuses on the gross sins in the Catholic faith, but it persists as much of not more in other denominations as well.

There are too many bad apples in church leadership, who are living proof of the distressing and vast silence. With too many seminaries vying for financial support and for students, the quality of today's divinity student reflects the culture.

According to recent research on sexual abuse and sexual violence, there is extreme pressure coming from church leadership against calling the horrid truth in their own communities. Of course, the situation is real. If you preach, you know the audience to whom you are preaching. It is comfortable and easy for the ordained clergy to put on impressive clerical garb and preach poetic sermons. It is much harder to be prophetic to "talk" with our congregations about the future of our children, our cultural norms, and whether the church is a place of safety. Most church leaders do not think they are equipped to take on the weight of these questions for their people. And most really are not prepared. Who has been prepared? Who would have the will and patience to spend 40 years after high school in serious study? I did. How? While I was earning nine degrees, I also served in ministry. Each training and education prepared me to earn my living by writing, counseling and therapy, as well as preaching. Our culture dictates who can do psychotherapy (soul healing) as it must.

Many physicians, psychologists, and licensed mental health counselors guide people into their versions of what our best version of ourselves are developed without guidelines. Life is always teaching us lessons. The most difficult life struggle is something we do not realize such as the elephants in the room: domestic sexual violence and sex trafficking.

God treasures every child, youth, and adult created in God's own image. Ministry begins by caring enough to get involved. Pay attention. When you observe a young girl, who is dressed provocatively and appears tube under control of an older man, see where she lives and call the authorities or a hotline. Most live where they work. They rarely travel alone. They will not speak for themselves.

They show body language of one living in fear. Most have been drugged and abused. We must open our eyes. It is all around us.

We must not slam the door to the problem by being of help. Mother Teresa said, "If you can't do great things do little things with great love. If you can't do them with great love, do them with a little love. If you can't do them with a little, do them anyway. Love grows when people serve."

The Hebrew Scriptures contain particularly hair-raising texts of terror, including the rape of Tamar in II Samuel 13:1-22, and the abuse of the unnamed concubine in Judges 19. The estranged husband finally offers his concubine to a mob who rapes her and beats her until she dies.

People who finally escape an abusive relationship have tried ten times or more. Leaving is a difficult option. It ends in economic hardship, cultural stigma, and the silence of the church.

A college student said, "I have never heard a sermon about sexual violence or sexual trafficking. I have never heard a preacher pray about it. I have never seen an education class about it." We dare not take the student's challenge to the heart of the Good News.

One of the hardest sermons one could preach is on this sexual violence. It is so difficult to stand in front of a congregation and talk about it. There will be people with unbelievable stories. They glare in frozen silence about being sexually abused in the home, during a high school relationship, on a college campus, or in the home where they live now. They cringe as they may have been old by a religious leader that they can never leave an abusive marriage because they would be breaking their sacred vows.

It is so essential to speak the Word of God now because too often in past years, religious traditions have been used to defend abuse, to bind victims to marriage commitments that are undermined by so much violence. Such congregations encourage people to "offer up" their suffering rather than change and repent for the conditions that cause it. Breaking the silence is essential because shining a light of the reality of distorted sexuality is critical in the creation of pathways to safety for the victims.

This is so essential because we are violating the love of God, and keeping victims from finding their way out. It is essential because naming sexual distortions as evil can help society to insist on making perpetrators accountable.

In some communities, Christians join with Jewish people, and Muslims to speak out publicly of this need. What can we specifically do? We can at least offer sessions for faith leaders, workshops for youth, and initiatives to help men and women who are victims. Religious based coalitions must join with professional service providers and law enforcement to change the culture around sexual distortion.

Of course, sexuality and spirituality includes forgiveness. But forgiveness does not free anyone from the consequences of mistreating another person. As ministers of joy to the world, we preach, teach, and write because if we keep silent, if we ignore the human cost and spiritual degradation of this evil, then we are failing the people whom we have been called to serve. We must speak out because if we speak up, we can help transform the world, healing the wounds that are so much before us. This speaking will bring us closer to the kind of place I believe that God intended for us.

I would be failing in my own piece of breaking the silence if I did not attempt to give some specific guidance. It is a sad failure that not all pastors realize that one third of the women sitting in the pews have been silent victims of sexual distortion. Some of the men in the congregations have been victims as well. Those who well know the horrifying statistics, but simply refuse to do anything.

Christianity is about serving the God of love who made all people with dignity and value. Jesus honored and respected women and resisted violence. Our youth need help and guidance to identify and avoid abusive relationships. Churches need to challenge any theology in the church that demeans women or condones sexual violence. We must educate ourselves on the issues of healthy relationships.

Prayers are an important and essential tool as we speak about healing for survivors of sexual distortion. We have plenty of biblical material to preach about rape, sexual violence, and human trafficking. Every church staff member and anyone who will be working with children and youth should be required to get child abuse prevention training.

Church groups can offer clothing, toothpaste, and other living supplies for women's shelters. Talks with youth should clearly know that consent is not negotiable.

Take the guidance of professional therapists who tell us that marital or couples counseling can increase the risk of danger for the victim. Recommend individual counseling sessions.

Do support a victim or survivor and believe them. I recommend responding to a sexual distortion story with compassion and belief. Those giving false accusations are small. Psychological damage is the result of casting doubt on the story. Keep in mind that sex abuse is well hidden, and it happens in the homes where you least expect it.

It is a scourge as old as the ages, yet sexual violence is fresh in the headlines.

Given the morality and virtue idealists associate with culture and faith, we still expect that congregants would be safe from abuse. Our critics could make a legitimate case that some traditions in church culture contribute to this problem. Pastors shy away from addressing this disturbing evil from their pulpits or their counseling roles.

Silence is the most important form of complicity. This book is my own attempt to serve as minister of joy to the world to mobilize pastors to preach against sexual violence inside and outside our churches. Children and women deserve to live free from terror and violence.

There are numerous things the local church can do. We must not continue to be passive bystanders in the face of abuse. Leaders can do an assessment of the congregation's current response. Welcome people who have been sexually abused to your church. Create a weeklong event to emphasize child and sexual abuse. Preach on it. Always do background checks on people who will work with our children. Develop a support group for adult victims of sexual abuse.

Chapter Seven

He Had Sex with Someone Else

How do we relate sex to love? The sexual experience is different for everyone. Enjoying it means how to make the best of lifestyles. A traditional, predictive perspective on life and sexuality need not result in sexual extinction through over control. Knowing one's best hours, seasons, and places for love, selecting the music, and readying the body and soul are factors that suit seekers' best dreams.

Romantic and passionate lovers are sensitive and deeply thoughtful. Immature sexual action is unrealistic, painful, and mostly self-destructive, but it feels immensely good. Realistically, the sexual experiences a rite of passage not only in the days of our youth, but through every life crisis as we live on into older age.

Sex is something adults do. Whether orgasm, ejaculation, or perfect touches and moves occur. there is an elation in these spontaneous joyful times. Ordinary people ask, married couples ask, even psychiatrists and professional ask, in private about the mysterious rapture. Can it feel that way again? Is there anything better?

Has any person on this earthly journey even been completely faithful? Even President Jimmy Carter admitted that he had sinned sexually through lust. Faithfulness asks far more than avoiding sexual contact with a third person. Within the boundaries of committed love and concern, we observe each one's needs are unique. The church gives just basic guidelines for faithfulness.

Adultery is another serious matter. Oh, what pain comes when a spouse realizes that "he had sex with another person."

It has the same tragic result in every culture. Sexual intercourse with any person who is not one's spouse is adultery.

In our culture adulterers lie and say there is no one else. They are eligible for marriage. "And no one can ever love you like I can." sparks hope. Sexual energy based on lies is a double injury. People create their own emotional environment. The church today does not stand for sexual monogamy. Culture is so strong humans are pushed away into abuse of the body, the temple of the Spirit of God himself.

But during unhappiness and poverty and straying from God encourages people to lift the lid off their sexual needs and urges. Today's media urges us to consider our sexual desires as sexual rights. So, adultery becomes attractive and inviting.

Couples begin their relationship with caring, love, commitment, and passion. When they meet, they never think the passionate fire of their love will ever diminish. But suddenly, the signs appear. There is a change in your spouse's attitude toward you. Faults are express about most anything. Walls crumple right before your eyes. Certainly, you did not grow ugly. Your once funny jokes now lack the steam to pull off laughter. Somebody totally new has become the yardstick for judging you. Moments are secrets you once cherished, but are not treasures anymore. Comparison enters in. You suddenly begin to compare your relationship with somebody else. This frustrates the joy in your relationship. So, adultery and lust enter the mind. It is never good to compare your relationship with one somebody else is in. This affects any relationship. It is better to acknowledge that each one has strengths and weaknesses. If you become prone to use another relationship as a measuring stick for your own, you will clearly know how it is hurting your relationship.

This human temptation causes one to think their lover is inferior. Comparing your spouse to another just like them shows your spouse what you crave as a new standard. This new fantasy person brings beauty and attraction you cannot match or meet up to even if you tried harder. So, they now are hurt and thinking they are inferior. Comparing robs them of the joy they had had in the relationship.

The next step brings distrust and betrayal. From being so loved to be put on a scale of comparison side by side another who was never in the picture creates total discomfort, distain, and distrust not only for your lover but for the opposite sex.

Joylessness and lack of peace come so there are no more smiles. Anxiety, nervousness, and body ills come, and sometimes you keep it locked within yourself. All this frustrates your love.

Unwanted hate for your rival begins to swell in you. That person may have directly or indirectly lowered your happiness level. Happiness and joy are essential in any relationship for it to thrive. In my marital counseling, that when you compare your relationship with others, you are only seeing them at their best. You are not getting a realistic picture of who or what they really are. Your eyes deceive you as you see a small fraction of the relationship and probable dynamics. Jesus said it bluntly, in saying it is better to pluck out your eyes then for your whole body to go to hell. This was an effective metaphor, but we get the point.

Building stable institutions is not the focus of writers and actors. Sexual satisfaction is the lure. Any human being becomes conscious of sex and the potential to satisfy desires.

Today we live in a cultural atmosphere that enables us to fly off to exotic places. Affluent people can pay for expensive lunches and hotel rooms. The reason the Sexual Revolution is so strong is that we now have the pill. So secretive adultery Is within the reach of more of us than ever before.

Marriages that are based on high erotic desire soon drive people outside marriage just for love alone to the hot flames of passion that have turned into hostile resentment.

A young adult woman shared her story. Her husband of her four children told her and the kids that he did want to be married to her. He was not kind. It was as if he was a different person. Wild and screaming, my lifetime love left and there appeared an ugly stranger. He looked so cold, cunning, but serious.

He had planned this family gathering as an ambush. He declared that he was not happy. He said he had not been happy for several years. He never was attracted to me. He said our sex life was a poor joke. There was no love. He said he did not want to spend more of his time with me. She said she realized that their sexuality was never passionate.

I just thought he has gone crazy. Still one very single day, he would continue to assure me of how little he thought of me. Separation or divorce had never entered her mind. Her family and her church were dead against it. Her heart and soul were broken. As she cried with painful tears, the reality began to sink into her unbelieving mind. This just could not happen. Our connection with each other, our whole marriage was a lie. She said that she had worried about many things. She had had to spend much time with the kids. Her take was that he never gave her reason to be concerned. There never was a focus on our sex lives. I just felt our sexuality was like everybody else's, she admitted. There was little affection that he gave to her. At church, we had attended a seminar on love languages. When they described the language of touch, we just assumed that touch was not his love language.

She had noticed that his parents never hugged or kissed or even smiled much. She wanted to fully accept him as he was. She imagined that his coldness was the pattern of his family. They created four beautiful kids, but there never any joy in their sex lives. She always assumed that he did love her.

What a shocking thing to hear when your mate says, "I do not love you." He wounded me further as he said, "I am not attracted to you. It was a mistake for us to marry." She had never suspected that he was having sexual relations with someone else.

The question that she and we ask is why? Some of our churches would dismiss it as human lust or degeneration. Her husband had bottled up restraint and discovering his sexual desire. Of course, humans have always had sexual drives. No man or woman is a stranger to lust. The reasons for infidelity are as unique as each couple must endure.

Our social environment, the atmosphere we breathe, no longer supports sexual faithfulness. Most couples who are active in their local congregations resist society's pressures. The media, the professionals, the sellers of most anything encourages couples to take the lid off their sexual needs and urges.

Our current atmosphere puts a premium on sexual fulfillment. The culture tells us that there is no fulfillment or oneness without sexual satisfaction.

The stories that run through the gamut illustrate there is less security or stability and people are pressured into asking questions about their own sexual wants and needs. People once choose to marry for comfort, security, and responsible functions such as being good churchgoers or effective parents.

Today people do not stand for unromantic marriages. The anticipation and expectation is that we celebrate, cultivate, and passionately enjoy sexual life together. When and if the marital experience grows dull or frustrating., some decide that marriage is not, after all, romantic enough. The cold ashes of resentment fan the flames of passion. Infidelity has never been easier. And it never has been so encouraged.

Nobody gets involved in adultery for any single reason. As pastors and therapists, we review the dynamics of conflicting needs and drives.

Deep anger pushes couples toward acts that punish the person toward whom the anger is directed. The one who has unresolved anger for personal failures. These people may have an anger disorder. The angry man or woman has not fallen in love with a third person. She is falling in anger against the spouse to be comforted in anger by another. She now has clout as a woman who is always providing, always faithful, and always extending herself to care for his needs while sheets little emotional or sexual satisfaction. The women and men who are blessed with affluence and equality, demand every spouse to have impossible excellence, be a rich provider a tender helper, the imaginative and passionate lover, the sturdy pillar, and a host of conflicting perfections. They insist on the impossible in a world of imperfect people. Most live in a fantasy.

Self-deprecation creates pressure toward adultery. People judge themselves for seeing themselves as failures. This low opinion causes condemnation for impossible demands. Shame and guilt are like the mafia of the mind. Most never talk about their blemishes within their marriage. They go seeking one who does not know them. They then choose someone much worse than themselves. Married to an abusive alcoholic, they will choose another alcohol addict.

Trying to make an escape from the boredom of children, in-laws, husband, and the whole life situation leads to running towards adultery. This kind of internal pressure is not a need for love or even sex, but is a factor in the inability to take responsibility.

Staying men cite boredom, sexual deprivation from the wife, emotional lack and his need for a lively counterpart. Men are turned on by powerful, aggressive females who bring an emotional charge into his life. These well-dressed, free of boundary women, offer something enticing. It is not that he has no sexual release, but he thinks he needs a woman who can aggressively feed more life into himself. This might and does involve self-doubt or perhaps unequal growth. His chosen wife may have supported him in this desire to become a valued professional with degrees from expensive graduate programs. His wife has been stunted in her growth. He may find a woman at his workplace, who brings out new facets inside himself that excite him. Inside himself, he is waiting for some woman to pry loose any barriers.

Creeping old age is a factor for women. Attractive, radiant women are pressured toward adultery when they are possessed with the thought they are losing their youthful attractiveness. This haunting anxiety has been conditioned by the culture to prize the gift of sexual glow.

Rough and dry skin, roundness to the stomach, sagging necks and cheeks cause them to consider the mirror and exclaim, "It's over. I'm not young anymore I look awful and it's only going to get worse."

A woman now sees vivid images of losing herself and her important relationships. With healthy spiritual insight, and the assurance that God sees her as the most loving lovely person she has ever been and that God was pleased with her.

So, a vision of the atmosphere for the joyful congregation is to talk about and with aging women whose looks might be crumbling into dust, but a woman growing in beauty. As she sees her image as God sees her, she will bear fruit as a woman of wisdom who reflects the bright light in every stage of life.

Dealing with the whole life from birth to death is the stuff of "the joy of the Lord."

Do you really want your church to talk better about sex? I am entranced by the research of Shawn Warner-Garcia. She is part of the movement to bring joy to the Church and our world. She has been collecting data on faith and sexuality among Christians in the United States.

Her research shared at the general assembly of 2017 of the Cooperative Baptist Fellowship made us feel as if we had just had an intimate, spiritual, and satisfying conversation with a knowledgeable and Christ-filled person.

Most of my thousands of hours of professional therapy involved a psychiatric diagnosis. Most therapy involved no perceived destination. I have found that in married life, there are predictable times when sexual infidelity occurs. These involved stress, loss, and joylessness.

Infidelity feasts on when a man or woman travels extensively alone, is depressed by perceived failure, changing of jobs or occupations, or are bored by monotony, or perhaps worn out with dull overwork.

The early years of retirement challenge older adults. If these experiences are happening in the life of one partner, the other becomes vulnerable to adultery. They need to be part of a calling together are they are pleased with their work to not succumb to temptation.

As an actively retired therapist, I now use life coaching in family ministries. Some events fall within predictable timetables. Some possibilities related to extramarital adventures include times of be bereavement, especially the death of a parent. Some comes from the empty nest as children leave for college. Pregnancy and childbirth, accident or a mate's illness, and the stressful events such as buying a home or a major change in lifestyle has been revealed during healing therapy. One reason the church needs to be involved in ministry to and from older adults is that when confronted by the process of aging is that the silence about lifetime sex has been ignored. After many years of marriage, couples no longer can cope with dissatisfactions that lead to the panacea of an affair.

Coaching or counseling can uncover reasons such as "have we deserted one another through attention to children, jobs, sick parents, or other responsibilities? Are you angry? Is this angry energy because of insecurity? Characteristic behavior in life resembles that in sex.

Another factor is retaliation. It occurs as a substitute for marital love. Soul healing therapy enables a couple to reach a point where they see working together on their sexuality as a new challenge. There is frustration in living with an asexual, cold, inadequate person who cannot change.

If the Church is to bring joy to the world, people must be trained to ask routinely about sex lives. Even physicians say, "Would that not be too embarrassing? I cannot imagine talking so personally? "Medical students are taught to ask about hearing, vision, headache, chest pain, digestion, back pain, appetite, leg pain, arm pain, breathing, bowel movements, urination, sores, bites, but questions concerning orgasm, erection, ejaculation are rarely asked. My brother is a family pediatric physician. Professors at Vanderbilt Medical School tell me questions about sexuality are routine now. There is no greater discovery to the process of living and dying than sexuality.

And another reason the Church must break this silence is that statistics show that extramarital sex increases in later decades. Perhaps older adults become uninhibited and free sexually. In my work as a senior and doing ministry with them reveals greater losses than we have ever talked about or imagined. So, they deeply desire an intimate bonding.

Let us pray and have the courage to be spiritual and "in the joy of the Lord as our strength," as we give needed insights on human relationships. People do not need a sex manual or a history of sex, and those who live with the human Jesus will find help and surprising joy. The Church will be the only source for us to demystify some of the most misunderstood issues.

Chapter Eight

Silence and the Continuing Sexual Revolution

Most people think the Sexual Revolution is now completed. The church breathes a sigh of relief. Others continue to regret that this new found understanding of our sexual selves. Society has now reversed the excesses of the sexual experimentation.

The mystical sensations that women reported during those decades of revolution included a sense of timelessness, a letting go, a strangely warm quiet mind. Many women love swimming to keep trim and in shape. After a half mile swim, women report a quiet state of mind that she reaches when making love is like the feeling she has when swimming her laps.

When first diving into the pool, her muscles feel coiled and tense. It is a strain to move in the water. After a while, her body feels loose and free, and the soothing water feels soft. Slicing through the heavenly softness becomes effortless. I am now swimming with my crystal-clear mind.

"When I have sex, I become more physical. I am emotionally excited, so I turn my body on," she reports. Becoming lost in the moment, she enjoys a clear mind.

We read and hear that society wants a return to the old family values. Some of the gains felt by the unhappy, sexually oppressed have suffered from the backlash. Silent response declares that the people welcome the backlash. People continue to pray and yearn for a continued sex revolution when spirit and body, soul and mind are not enemies.

We wonder how creatures such as us, stuck as we are with demanding and persistent sex urges, should live. We ask God ourselves how we are doing today. We want to know how our sexual selves fits into our brief years of our earthly journey and how this fits into God's story and purpose.

Saint Paul's words give us some insight. In Philippians, he wrote in chapter one, verse nine, "I pray that your love may abound more and more, with knowledge and discernment, so that you may approve what is excellent."

There has been several Sexual Revolutions in history. The one of the past decades brought deep change. The term "revolution" implies widespread change. The churches including those called "mainline" still held traditional views. The sex revolution in the 1920's was one factor in the rise of fundamentalism.

Because the sex revolution was centered on college students, some leaders Saw a need to do campus ministries. Chester Sword was a Southern Baptist who was an older adult and lived in a crippling condition, but millions of students heard him gladly as he broke the silence of the church. One of the most influential ministries of the Sunday School Board of the Southern Baptist Convention was the Student Ministries Department.

The churches in every group believed that they could not remain silent. Among the majority in the culture, sex became more socially acceptable outside the boundaries of marriage.

The movie industry added to the problem with adult erotic films. With expensive and successful promotions, millions viewed them. The pill was a tool that gave women an affordable way to avoid pregnancy. This opened the gates to the opportunity for sex anywhere, any time, and with no boundaries. The pill gave women control of their futures. With no fear of pregnancy, they could finish their education and ultimately gaining profession careers.

What was called the Moral Majority noted that women's sexual freedom was cause for regressions in the quality of life. Research proves that sexually transmitted diseases, teen pregnancy, and divorce all have risen dramatically. Marriage has declined by one-third and divorce has more than doubled. Children living in single parent families has tripled adding to the poverty, unhappiness, and miserable existence. The only guidance offered was, "don't get yourself raped."

Gabriele Kody said, "Abandonment of Christian sexual morality is the core of the Church's self-secularization." The church discovers more egg on her face because of the failure to speak out in the face of grievous injustices.

The Third Reich gained evil and disrespectful powers that is like the metaphor of boiling a frog in water. In the beginning, people in Germany may not have voted for the Nazi Party, kicking and screaming, but wanting relief from economic depression and loss of national pride. During most of these historic times, the Church tried to divert its eyes from evil and resisted the truth. The fact remains that any of the few resisters faced enormous opposition especially when anyone attempted to open the eyes of their fellow believers.

Christian spokesman such as Martin Luther King in our time, and Dietrich Bonhoeffer in the Nazi era, were killed like Jesus forespeaking truth and joy. King said, "We will have to repent in this generation not merely for the vitriolic words and actions of the bad people, but for the appalling silence of the good people."

Just as the political leaders of Germany and the United States of America used the phrase "the do-noting government, "we could say the "do-nothing Church" refuses to reveal any moral insight that is above and against the grain in the face of severe injustice and evil.

During these times of the prevailing worldly kingdom, the perception of the church's abdication exceeds all other eras and places. Political movements such as Nazism, as well as slavery, disrespect, and all other aspects of fallible sinners, the church acts out of agendas outside the directions toward the Kingdom of God.

The biggest issue today is that we are in a more existential crisis. Once Again, we live in a world of political ideology that influences the heart of the church and attacks the core mission of God in Christ. This is Not some external threat, but an attack on itself, and has left it helpless in the spiritual wars of our age. Revolutions have destroyed the church's own defenses, and it is not unified enough to make a difference.

Political parties claim to control and exercise state power. Many are really members of a political party that has become their church. Today's sexual radicals push on with their demands on not only who desire freedom of religion. The genius of our church and state separation is honorable so that no kind of religion can rule at the whim of the majority.

The silent minority of the church who are among the "few that find it, "And that will result in crushing the authority of the church altogether. Our churches and institutions to remain asleep. We must be a part as those who are finally waking up.

We listen to the complaints about how Christians are despised and marginalized. Many find the perceptions of sexuality as a divisive issue. We camouflage this by displays of compassion for the poor. The world then hates the church even more. Nazism, communism, and other evil movements took over with very little opposition.

Hunger, poverty, and taxes in the world's most affluent nations does not result from lack of wealth or the generosity of people. Overindulgence of sexual freedom results in turning poor women and their children into welfare addicts. This results in an increase in power by governments. The result is that the world notes the shallowness of our compassion.

The gospel message coupled assistance to the poor with biblical morality. The poor, the middle class, and the rich are sinners and have responsibilities. Sinners can then be re-labeled "victims."

When I served as pastor of six congregations in the Max Meadows Circuit of the United Methodist Church in the Blue Ridge Mountains of Virginia, where many citizens lived on welfare.

One affluent member sought to build a new prison with the lure of "good paying new jobs." The majority and most of the men opposed it. They well knew that most of those sent to prison were males. They noted that they felt like easy targets for accusations that they claimed were fabricated. Besides drug offenses, men were put into prison for sexual harassment, rape, sexual assault, sexual manipulation, sexual this and sexual that.

Courage and the conversion to "the joy of the Lord" for a life of happiness in Christ was my focus. Spiritual goodness and the polishing of a complete soul using sexual energy for good was new to them.

I was advised not to deal with sexuality for "the sake of unity in the United Methodist Church." How does a pastor avoid the formidable grip on personal lives, on the community, and evolving church structures?

The culture opposed dealing vigorously with sexuality because it is viewed as incidental or inappropriate to "the life of the spirit." I believe it threatened the entrenched male power. In my experience, most district superintendents, the bishop, and most appointed pastors were males. Many leaders feared divisiveness and the consequences for the church's Unity. So most lived with reactive and not proactive ministry. My approach was a low key one. I listened to the youth who were yearning for the church to support and to stand up for them. I heard the voices of single adults who felt avoided and even condemned by the church. I had Christ's words of hope for the disabled and the aged who said they found so much joy from the faith they followed.

What youth and young adults call the "juicy stuff" can we shared if we are willing. Sexuality is a gift for communion. For some successful sex education classes, the goal is to observe sex as a human need for pleasure and release. But biology of sex is a small part of it.

Sexual satisfaction is to be united spiritually as well as physically. Sex creates delight and pleasure. Creation and grace are taught as a spontaneous and ecstatic playful experience that nobody should be ashamed of.

Jesus wanted the church to serve in unity. Too many congregations are polarized and paralyzed. Bringing joy to the world requires church filled with a spirit of joy. We divide ourselves into fundamental and conservation against the liberals and progressives, the rural and the city, the right and the left, the poor and the rich, the good and the bad. So, we do not risk the courage to be leaders of the faith, centered in character, and expressed in joyful action. We must preach the Word of God with the Good News that connects with Christ to make a difference in our homes, our churches, our communities, the nation, and the world.

Christ gave the Great Commission for us to be compassionate with afresh and open-minded biblical based perspective. The message must be plain spoken, and yet responsible. The spirit of God is calling all of us to join to plan a new sexual revolution before it's too late.

Chapter Nine

Has God Picked Someone Special for Me to Marry?

When my daughter was seventeen, I took her shopping for a special white dress for her National Honor Society initiation.

As we shared an intimate Daddy-Daughter conversation, she asked, "Has God picked someone special for me to marry?"

My answer was the same that I would give to any young women today. "Yes, God has created someone just for you." I told my daughter that God does not always give us just one option. God gives us free will to choose. Quite a few Christian men would be a perfect match. Patience, discernment, prayer, and even studying about personality types, birth order, love language, or use your intuition. The answer will be revealed.

Marriages are not made in heaven. Marriage requires work, nurturing, patience, inter-dependence as marriage requires spirituality, commitment, and compromises with these earthly kits and worldly glue. If the couple together follows God's guidance, there is high prediction of times where joy explodes, and each supports the other's personal purpose.

We live our lives from a temporal point of view. Jesus told us there will be no marriages in heaven. God directs us from an eternal viewpoint. Our creator designed us to let our God live within our beings proven by the fruit of the Holy Spirit so we reflect love, joy, peace, patience, kindness, goodness, faithfulness, gentleness, and self-control. As we let God control our lives, whatever choices we make, whatever circumstances we find ourselves in, God will continue the creativity to accomplish the Lord's purpose in our time on earth and forever.

Our choice of a marriage partner will change the entire course of our lives. We are never in a place on earth where God cannot accomplish the creator's will for our lives. We can never place ourselves beyond God's reach. We can only refuse to be touched. Our own attitudes toward God are the only barriers to doing what is desired for each one of us.

Our Divine Lover sends soft, gentle whispers, the flutter of angel wings penetrating trough the quiet times if we are listening. The most important consideration for connecting with another human being centers on the question, "Will this person help me to remain open to God's leadership in my life? "

Marriage is not a static bonding. Couples are alive with potential for change. Our Maker continues to make changes within us. The truth is that two are stronger than one by themselves. By God's mysterious power will weld us together for glory and joy. Marital happiness is not a problem to be solved, but a mystery to be lived.

The Bible informs us that "in this world you will have trouble." Read John 16:33. With the joy of the Lord as our strength, couples live through many sorrows, pain, loss of jobs, sickness of all kinds, but they live in a happiness and peace that defies human understanding. God has promised to be with us during our troubles. Our Maker uses these times to make us stronger people.

As couples turn to God in times of difficulty, the Lord gives strength and enrichment. When we decide to marry, marry for life, and realize how hard we shall have to work at harmony. And in the final years, after we have shared intimate thoughts and experiences, after we have weathered all that life will bring us, your lives together will delightfully prove to each of you there could be anyone more suited to your needs and more fun to be with as you discover surprising joy.

Leo Boskalis taught the psychology of love at UCLA. During a class lecture he said that we are one-winged angels who live to be best version of ourselves only when we choose to be intimate with another person. Christians agree that love is the most important aspect of living. We read I Corinthians 13 at weddings. In our culture, we obsess about the concept of love. We use falling in and out of love. Our struggles include getting stuck with the wrong person, murdering each other over love, doing something dangerous or illegal with it. We are hypnotized emotionally. He experiences a type of love seizure.

In my Visionquests for Joy, we emphasize that we need joy in love before we can find the joy of sex. But our distortions of love create a serious barrier to finding someone special to embrace.

Love is not a feeling and sex is not a sport. Love is not one of our emotions. Counselors and parents insist that what our youth feel is not "real." We blame and cite the hormones.

Dorothy Tennon invited a new word "limerence." To her, the word Means a vacillation between elation at a perceived reciprocity of feelings and an underlining discomfort when the feeling is not returned.

Love is not a feeling. It is a commitment, a passion, and an intimacy. Love is being bonded by our will, intention, and thinking through what is happening. In human sexuality, passion is a combination of many emotions and a physical longing within a desire to be a part of someone else's life, and ultimately to join physically.

Love does not include jealousy of your lover, feeling lucky that you have been accepted, or that your life would have no worth without your chosen one. If that is what describes your love, it will be gone in a few months.

When we break the silence about sex and love, our youth feel freed to ask the questions. The one I hear most every time is, "How do you know when you're in love?" I always honor the question and respect the young person.

I say something like, "If you think you are in love, you are without a doubt into something. You might be in love or you could be in lust. Lust is a distraction. Lust takes time away from your friends, school, home, church, or involvement in community life. If it's love you will become more involved with many people. You will use most of your energy for your school, family, and spiritual life.

The Silence of the Church

If it is lust, it will not last. Lust means you're on a quick high with your brain chemicals.

Most of the love songs and especially country music lyrics are limerence songs. If our past traditions attempted to establish a sexless love, then the 2000's brought on loveless sex. The result has been a massive failure.

During a retreat on in an intimate camp setting, couples talked about who wanted sex, who wanted love, who needed more love for better sex, or better sex for more love. The conclusion is that both sex and love are essential for a complete and full life. "The talk" need not be the information from a sex manual, but a reflection on sexuality as touching a shoulder, cuddling a child or a parent, exchanging a glance, a warm hug, are each one vital as sexual acts that complete the oneness that bonding brings.

Campus ministry reveals that most college students believe that love is something that just happens. They think that people have pre-planted love seeds that just sprout spontaneously in response to a person who stimulates them. Love overwhelms people. They admit that some of their experiences include the worst thing that even happened to them, but they could not help themselves.

We made the decision to love. It is a conscious, thought out choice. Love is not helpless nor naïve. Nobody is a willing victim. We can attach with many people, worthy or not worth your time and energy. We can choose to bond with only one person at a time. Television shows such as "The Bachelor," perpetuates a lie that one can be in love with many different people. And that love exists at the same time.

The gift of sexual energy spent on bonding is an invested energy. That limited energy is spent on one bonding. It is never available for two attachments.

If we think that we must search for one singular person chosen just for us, we stress ourselves to believe a lie that limits love. We naturally have sexual attraction for many people. God's idea of bonding is that life should not depend on finding the right person, but on being the right person. Ask yourself, "Would you fall in love with you? "

Love is a commitment, but in our life journey, love does not last forever. Love is limited by divorce, death, illness, or long separations. Loving itself is infinite, even if humans are not. Our limited time brings our choice to break the bond. Nothing will cancel the memory, the love traces, but we must now change the relationship because of the loss of the physical presence of the loved person.

That love continues to live in us, so that we hold the same desires, the same spiritual yearnings, and the same priorities as God. The personal experience of the love of God for ourselves gives us new unexplainable strength. The Holy Spirit continues to dwell inside us until we die, and go onto live forever. We need an experience with God to change our entire life. We remain the fruit of our past life, the total of everything that we lived from the moment we were born.

Every human being we have encountered, every event we attended, every choice we made, is deeply engraved in us, even if our memories are lost, our body remembers.

Grief and loss are inseparable from our journey. We cannot accept the gifts life brings us without the losses. When we love, we give new life. When we love another, we trust and reveal the loved one's value, beauty, and the truths of life. Some may become afraid of love as our culture views it as a weakness or something linked only to our sexuality.

Love is never easy. Joy comes upon us in moments, ordinary moments. We miss joy when get too busy chasing the extraordinary. Culture invites us to live small, but when we talk to people who have great losses, joy is not a constant. We place in our memories the ordinary moments. "I miss our ice cream bars as we enjoyed a sporting event. "I miss his silly giggle when he reacted to the local news." "I miss his anger at the computer when it could not store his best little poem written just for me."

As anybody who lived through pain, loss, or tragedy how their struggle cultivated more compassion and love for others, they tell us to never shrink from the joys of your loved one. Celebrate each day with gratitude. Be thrilled that your parents are still healthy. When we honor what we have, we honor what we lost.

Salvation comes as we lean into "the joy of the Lord as our strength, "We turn every opportunity as a surprising possibility for joy. We will create resilience to unhappy times, and we will create hope for strugglers everywhere.

Joy becomes part of who we are. And when bad things appear— and they always do—we are stronger.

When our chosen lover dies, we become completely frozen. We might not have any sexual feelings for some time. The loss of sexual identity seems insignificant besides the loss of a person. You now go everywhere alone. We miss a loving arm around our shoulders. We lose someone special that we have been free to confide in. And when there is a joke or funny moment, somebody to laugh with.

In this frozen condition, people describe physical sensations, times our chest hurts, our joints ache, our eyes become are never clear. Swallowing and breathing are difficult. There is a permanent dull ache in the stomach.

If it's the woman who is left behind, her periods may suddenly stop. Or they will become painful. Now death takes everything away as if we are now well outside humans. The feelings are beyond happiness or frozen sadness.

There is no connection. We feel like we are cut off from others. Talking about your grief threatens others like a highly contagious disease. You become unable to face people. When we grieve, the other person still seems not to have really gone. As we clasp our grief, we hold on to the reality of our lost person. We are afraid to get out as we just cannot bare Friends now must talk about difficult subjects, and even share our moments of shame. No person or group can learn to be more vulnerable or courageous on their own.

Our audience for this book is not only for church or non-churched people. We are all in this together.

Talking about this experience may even cause withdrawing from the children. Comfort may come for a woman with a hot bath or just lying in bed under a warm blanket. A grieving woman without a man becomes threat to other women Her female friends think she is exploiting male compassion. If she is attractive and a "suitable age,"she may be viewed as "available."

At such emotional times, it is normal to get angry with God. They are angry with themselves, with other people. and even with the one who died. The energy of anger can bring depression and guilt.

When and if erotic feelings return, the feelings come suddenly. They erupt in an uncontrollable time. And they come with profound guilt. The woman may now believe that she has no right to sexual pleasure. She might not think she is fully alive, now that her lover is dead.

The joy of going to bed with someone, not just for intercourse, but to be cuddled, to talk intimately, is what is missed, a widow said in a church grief support group. These community or spiritual groups can break the isolation to enable widows and widowers to communicate even if it is at a superficial level.

Some congregations organize Divorce Recovery groups, as a divorce is often worse than death. People cannot weep or express feelings. Divorce is another occasion for a deep freeze on emotions. The recovery group can help with the physical constrictions, or wanting to end the misery, live through the gradual thaw and come to life again. Those with strong spiritual beliefs report being spiritually stronger. The group can result in a new sense of self. Life brings unwanted experiences, especially when they involve that one special person who traveled with you. There is a world of struggling fellow humans out there who need to know happiness and joy. Another somebody special could well bless one's life much more than they could imagine. As John Wesley said, "The world is my pulpit." Facebook recently reported they have two billion customers. With about 7. 5 billion living on our planet now, it would not be unusual to connect with another person who lives and works on any of our seven continents.

The social media makes it possible to be in close touch with a special person with whom you will know the highest happiness and moments of joy. God has not quit working and communicating to his children. The choices are unlimited. And with God's guidance and grace, you will once again make a connection.

Chapter Ten

Feeling Life: Sexuality and Joy

Feeling life through sexuality was positive for the Hebrew people. They believed sex was entirely approved by God. Sexuality brought not only pleasure, but moments of sheer joy. They would be outraged at any suggestion that sex was unspiritual.

During Old Testament days, the faithful believed that God was personally present when husband and wife had intercourse. God showed his pleasure or displeasure by opening or closing the womb.

A new sex revolution will reveal the most lavish insight into human nature. Sexual attitudes, activities, even fantasies can reveal our honest character.

Harry Hollis oversaw family life concerns for the Christian Life Commission of the Southern Baptist Convention. He was my supervisor for my field education and clinical counseling work at Vanderbilt Divinity School.

Dr. Hollis helped me to see that sexuality of the highest feeling in life Is a natural part of our being. To live Christ-like the church needed creative methods and a willingness to fight for a healthy theology of sexuality. To deny that our bodies ever tingled with sexual desires is to deny what is basic about living. Foy Valentine served as the courageous head of the Christian Life Commission.

At the beginning worship for a Visionquests for Joy in a large congregation, the following prayer written by Harry Hollis was distributed among the participants. This prayer could be used in any congregation of any theological environment.

One question that always comes up when a church decides to break the current silence about sexuality is where can we find effective material on God's precious gift that can be used by parents, couples, children, youth or older adults in a church setting.

Pray this prayer that will amaze you. It is biblical, simple, provocative but comforting and filled with dignity. Pray it with me now.

> Lord, it's hard to know what sex really is. Is it some demon put here to torment me? Or some delicious seducer from reality? It is neither of these. Lord. I know what sex is. It is body and spirit. It is passion and tenderness. It is strong embrace and gentle hand holding. It is open nakedness and hidden mystery. It is joyful tears on honeymoon faces, and It is tears on wrinkled faces at a golden Wedding anniversary. Sex is a quiet look across the room, a love notes on a pillow, a rose laid on a breakfast plate, Laughter in the night. Sex is life, not all of life, but wrapped up in the meaning of life. Sex is your good gift, O God, to enrich life, to continue the race, to communicate, to show Me who I am, to reveal my mate, to cleanse through one flesh. Lord, some people say sex and religion don't mix, but your word says sex is good. Help me to keep It good in my life. Help me to be open about sex, and still protect its mystery. Help me to see That sex is neither demon or deity. Help me not to climb into fantasy of imaginary sexual Partners. Keep me in the real world to love the People you have created. Teach me that my soul does not have to frown at safer me to be a Christian. It is hard for many to say, "Thank God for sex." They need to know that sex and gospel can be linked together again. They need to hear the good news about sex. Show me how I can help them. Thank you, Lord, for making me a sexual being. Thank you for showing me how to treat others with trust and love. Thank you for letting me talk to You about sex. Thank you that I feel free to say, "Thank God for sex."

The worship leader then helped the congregation give praise to God for the gift of sexuality. What better place to celebrate human sexuality than church?

In our past, some churches have presented Christianity as an anti-sexual religion. This is flatly contradictory to the teaching of Jesus.

Why are we who know the joy of the Lord not free to celebrate the most important gift in all human life in the church?

Why does the church not take the responsibility for sex education in age-related retreats, creative worship, and in preaching the Good News?

Sexuality is the number one hang-up in therapy work. Too many continue to accept joyless communion through sex. Don't we understand that sex is a natural and essential part of our existence.

There are at least four simple questions in psychotherapy sessions that reveal most of the concerns of couples." Are you happily married? Does your spouse love you? What do you think about him or her? How do you feel about her or him? "

God is just as fascinated with our sexual lives as with our prayer lives. Our God is sexy. When our lives have no joy or happiness, God is not pleased.

Satisfied couples enjoy romance, hand holding, cuddling, and kissing. Women complain that men never do loving touching except during foreplay. Speak out for the joy of touching. Men can experience happiness and a time of joy with this kind of non-sexual touching.

Couples need for tender moments goes beyond actual love making. Some fall to sleep just after the act. When a man is having sex, his endorphins are in high levels. Almost immediately after ejaculation, men lose their erection and his system gears down.

For women, this phase will happen gradually. When a woman does not like Him falling asleep or starting to snore, wake him and tell him without putting him down. Let him fall asleep in your arms for a few minutes and then awaken him later.

Good intimate conversation is an aphrodisiac. Talking and feeling loved or taking a walk together before is a reassurance that they are in love and with each other mentally during these intimate moments. How couples treat each other out of bed influences the response in bed. Harsh language, hurtful words, rude tones, criticism, and inattentiveness closes enthusiastic passionate sex

Every time we have sex will not give us a deep joy. We set ourselves up for failure if that is always our expectation. Sometimes sex is just awkward, unsatisfying. We are humans, not machines. Sexuality is a spiritual communion, not a sport. An orgasm is not necessary. Sure, it is wonderful to experience orgasm, but sometimes it is better with loving foreplay. Communication is one of the best factors during love making. Silence speaks a multitude of love languages. When two bodies are intertwined as one, the deepness of the breath, the sound of your heartbeat, and the laughs or those unique sounds of satisfaction, are the only sounds that need to be heard.

Take responsibility for your own sexual pleasure. Sex is not something you do for or to another person. By paying attention to how we think, dream, and act when we are feeling life, we can tell who we are and what we believe. People with graceful and appealing sex lives enter it with prayer and meditative connection. It is most holy. Sex when you are committed to love never needs to involve pressure. There is magic of the love language of touch. Tantalizing thoughts instantly flood the mind when couples enjoy amorous, passionate sex between two people wrapped up in love. Loving bodies come alive. Individual bodies are clashing together to create an unpredictable, yet impressive reaction. This reaction is the chemistry of love. Signs of this emotional explosion are heavy breathing, lightheadedness, and a mystical spiritual mindset.

What kind of information do couples in a trusting, spiritual setting with others finally share? Some say they enjoy sex like they are enjoying music, viewing lovely art, or reading a helpful book. They speak of feeling a unique unity, as their life dreams are now falling into place. They report overwhelming passion that was strong enough to involve soul, blood, and reason that swept them into feeling that everything was right now as if nothing could go wrong again. They spoke of a timelessness, and they said that life should be like this forever.

James McReynolds

Sexual ecstasy has been overlooked or not allowed so long by ministers, theologians, and honest seekers that we wonder why every disciple of Christ can reach such a joy experience that they really do not mind sharing with others.

Too many have only experienced hasty, routine, anxious, and exploitative sex, and this hardly predisposes a person for anything. Few couples in our meetings could equate sex with religion. Those who shared their new insights had a sacred dimension. Those who shared felt peace and at one with themselves and all creation.

Harry Emerson Fosdick, pastor of the Riverside Church in New York, insisted that preaching was counseling in a group setting. He believed the spiritual awareness needed in joyful sexuality could be found in the church.

The most neglected sexual art is laughter. Laughter is what gives passionate couples laugh and that gives encouragement and even prolonged pleasure.

Sometimes a scream of delight sounds out the summit of our joy and a glory that we feel. If we silence it, we will never know the barrier we have passed.

Serious fearful people find it rare to laugh. Laughter fills our bellies. We breathe it out in bursts of amazing joy. Christians laugh with biblical concepts of dignity and God. God is sexy. So, our response to sex, as tart, music, or poetry lies in our emotions. Sex is best when it involves strong feeling. Joy comes at the peak of our divine pleasure. People are not created to be silent robots. Emotional overtones come in all human behaviors.

Sexuality is a spiritual blessing. The feelings that come after a joyous sexual experience are a new area for concern. This differs if after sexton a night, a weekend, or the rest of their lives is the expectation. Those who don't feel intimate as a foundation for sex may be ashamed of the feeling, so they avoid vulnerability afterward. Some just fall asleep, go get something to eat from the refrigerator, steep themselves in a book or in a television program, or repair the washing machine. Women lament, "He just turns over and falls asleep."

Some couples feel nothing after sex. Others are crushed when their lover leaves. Feeling or not feeling may be a key to breaking the silence. During the acute phase of joy, sex is experienced as wonderful.

Our culture and the church deals with high divorce rates, even with parents of young children, testifying to the early disillusion. Maybe if the sex were better, life together would be more attractive. The highest levels of happiness contain the desire to do more than satisfy. The level of satisfaction you receive from finally being with a partner who understands the depths and curves of your soul and mind will result in more than pleasure, but two people encountering the world, doing what the Creator designed for us.

There is no mystery in the reduction of sexual joy. If it remains at all among people bound to one another for better or worse, it would be a surprise for the host of couples who know in their soul that what they are doing is right and good. With God's guidance, you have confirmed to yourself that you are emotionally and spiritually linked to the person that is right for you. God's plan for sex is different from sex in general. There are no regrets to be made, and no feelings of shame or guilt.

Lovemaking with godly guidance and just having sex have opposite definitions on the intimacy scale. Sharing love is one of the most beautiful gifts that God's design for our human bodies will experience. Breaking the silence will enable the Church and God's world to crack the stigma of taboos related to sexuality.

Breaking the silence enables talk about hidden hurts and happiness. Without shame, we dare to communicate about love and how it can be expressed in sex. Sexuality has been oversimplified. We have too common taboos and inbuilt prejudices around how people of all ages feel and speak, about their earthly bodies. It is the feeling of joy in every aspect of life.

God designed your body as a wonderland. Allowing your chosen soul mate to navigate every part will fill your mind with deep appreciation and gratitude. You are the light in this person's world. When the two of you are intimate, your bodies create an explosion of astonishment that can never be created anywhere else.

Too many in and out of the Church are disturbingly superficial in reducing sex to an animal act damaging their humanity. When people struggle to find satisfaction in sex, many sinks in the quicksand and may even be joined with a joyless, unhappy person who falls with those traveling the road to ever-increasing frustration and gnawing emptiness. To fritter away your gift of sexuality on someone you are not committed to with love is to become like a person who burns hundred-dollar bills and cannot figure out why they are so impoverished.

Maintaining silence will certainly lead us to dangerously misinterpretations of our human cravings. We have a whole bunch of complex needs that some tend to naively think can be met with sex. The consequence of this mistake will be catastrophic. How do we communicate in a world that gets things horribly confused?

In the next chapter, we will discuss what it means to be one flesh. To be in one flesh is to experience a oneness in which the greatest joy is found in the highest happiness of the other. Our silence will cheat ourselves out of the fulfillment in which we were born into this brief time on earth to enjoy. Lust is a self-perpetuating cycle that becomes more intense as it continues. We must not fail to show that the driving force most sex addicts' compulsion is the desperate need for love. God has our best interests in his heart. When we crave for a relationship, we respond to our Creator's guidance like spoiled brats asked to eat their vegetables and not the candy. The consequences of casual sex cannot be undone. We can never create a new past. Of course, God and you can forgive any sin including our sexual ones.

Chapter Eleven
"The Word Became Flesh"

The first Christian believers had faith that God could become a human being. The world's take and even Christians living today cannot think that a holy God would ever take a human body. People of most world religions are offended by the teaching of the incarnation. Many cultures have a low understanding of the element of sexuality of the human body.

The story of salvation is that humankind as Jesus taught us that he was Just like us. except he lived a sinless life.

The body of Jesus was a real earthly body. The same organs that all people have inside their bodies, Jesus lived with too. Sincere people get really filled with anxiety as they comprehend the sexuality of Jesus. The historic doctrine of the Trinity to some equates to serving three gods. The fact that Jesus never married proves there is the possibility of being a sexual being without having genital sexual relationships.

Most books written to an audience of Christians or just plain folks is often bland and quite limited and thin, denying that sex is such an important part of human salvation. Human sexuality is not just having intercourse.

Jesus was given the mission to seek and save the lost. So, sexuality can be re-channeled. Of course, Jesus lived as a male among women. He felt the female touch of women as well as the hardy handshakes of men. Being a human being, certainly Jesus felt erotic feelings toward women. And he enjoyed the delights of female presence and friendship. Without his women supporters, he could not have completed his mission. He chooses twelve men to serve as his apostles, but the names of women are given, as well as their own ministries to the Savior of the World. The women did not run away when he endured the cross for the salvation of both men and women.

Women were attracted to Jesus in erotic ways. When ***Jesus Christ Superstar*** was presented in churches and large assemblies, the church became nervous. Jesus enjoyed the presence of Mary. One of the telling lyrics of the Christian musical, expressed her deep erotic feelings: "I don't know how to love him." Mary could only understand "love" as including genital sex. Her personal passion could not be contained. Mary had to learn how to love Jesus, collecting videos and dreams and imaginations of the goodness of sexuality. Culture in that day and today could imagine that Jesus was not inclined to make love to a woman for whom he felt love. Pious traditional feelings are offended at even the thought. Do these think Jesus the Savior of the world is not worthy of sex? So, if sexes unworthy for him, it is unworldly for humans as well. Jesus was among the first men to treat woman as equals. He cherished females as his intimate friends.

In Mark 10:5-9, it is recorded that Jesus broke the silence of the Jewish Tradition approved the arrogant right of husbands to get rid of their wives as they got rid of their cattle. He declared that sex had been planted into the Garden of Eden and that men and women should be sexually attracted to each other. He taught that sexuality was not a nasty product of sin, but the dynamic of God's creation.

Jesus believed sexuality is affirmed by the route that God took for the salvation of humanity. God has embraced the body life of us all in the incarnation and the resurrection. Salvation is not an escape from the demands or desires of human body. As part of our professions of faith that Jesus rose from the grave bodily is to make clear God's feelings about his "good" creation as body, mind, and soul persons.

God did not become a man to teach us how to get out of our bodies by any means. Now carefully read John 3:16. The resurrection of Jesus makes God's union with all humanity, affirming sexuality as part of our hope for the highest happiness and abundant joys.

Breaking the silence of the church means sex cannot not be left alone to find its release apart from the new being. This is new and very Good News. Recent church culture says that Christianity offers new controls for sexuality. So, all the church does is create stricter rules. And the powerful suppress sexuality with a new motive. Legalism is a reaction against healthy concept of salvation. Legalists cannot fence in sexuality to create hold on people. Paul wrote in his letter to the Galatians 5:1, "For freedom Christ has set us free." Everything in us must be set free.

Sexual freedom is misunderstood. Church culture has taught that freedom in Christ is freedom from sexuality. They interpret Paul's words to be free "from the desires of the flesh," by which the church has said that "desires" means "sexual desires." Casual distorted sexuality and repressed sexuality reduce sexuality to merely a biological function.

Satisfying sex brings human close to each other to share the most intimate exposure of ourselves in uncontrolled and spontaneous trust of one another.

We have lost touch with our deep inner joy that is natural to children. Salvation means to reconnect with "the joy of the Lord" as adults. God' salvation is an awakening that frees us to be more open with life's pleasures. "When I professed my conversion to Jesus and my fellow people, I was being rejuvenated and I experienced euphoric joy," said a person at one of our Visionquests for Joy.

This attitude is expressed in the prayer used at Alcoholics Anonymous meetings, "God, give me the serenity to accept the things I cannot change, the courage to change the things I can, and the wisdom to know the difference."

A female minister shared how she continued to remember her joy experiences. She recalled her wedding music. She felt the touch of her husband in his absence. In her life videos, she brings back the first time her man kissed her. She re-reads old love letters, valentines, and words from her personal journals, gaze on photos of a special trip as she allows herself to gently drift along with the sensations and images that emerge.

The mystery of our sexuality is part of the deep mysteries of life. The mystery and anxiety of sex cannot be revealed by quantitative measurements alone. That mystery of sex is the mystery of persons in encounter at every time they have sex. Yet so much is untapped.

Mystics, including thousands of Christians, experience an intuitive understanding of what the nature of reality includes in the moment. They find in the silence "the way things are." Theologians have been fascinated by mysticism. In sexually repressed times church leaders taught that it was immoral to think that sex could produce a feeling as elevated as mystics had described in spiritual quests by the religious monks.

Even if passionate sex is like mystical experience, few women really equated sex with religion. Something profound has happened to them, and it felt like an extremely sacred moment. The overwhelming sense of oneness that mystics report is the same feeling when they are communing with God filled their inner soul.

Those vulnerable and confident enough felt a compulsion to say that sexes God's gift brought them close to God, with deep inner peace, and mysterious oneness with themselves, their spouses and the world.

During a young adult retreat focusing on Heaven, a man shared that with a pleasurable sex life, he viewed life as worthwhile. He also said the experience was like a visit to heaven from which he returns. That heaven is a colony of the real thing that exists all the time all around us, always available for us for a short time at least.

The vulnerability shared during a spiritually enhancing conference said, "It was a moment of heavenly intervention. My wife and I were floating in an unbounded space filled with clear colors and such relaxing warmth. There were no boundaries between our bodies. We sensed a freedom. Our time appeared to both of us as timeless."

Ernest Hemingway used a phrase in the book, **For Whom the Bell Tolls**, "the earth moved." These three words sums up the sort of lovemaking most humans dream all their lives anticipating the rare

The Silence of the Church

experience. Several women through the years have used that phase, "the earth moved."

A young adult from California related that her intense joys in rebought images of water like the ocean shore, waterfalls, clouds, floating, wetness, the sweet smell of salt, and liquid fireworks. Sparks ignited in liquid form. Her description felt like God's gift at its best.

There is a spiritual connection beyond what most people think possible. With the spirit of Christ inside us, humans feel connected to the universe. Spiritual people can go far beyond conventional boundaries. Breaking the silence of sharing just how "good" God's gifts are, enables any of us to gladly strive for our full potential.

The same Jesus who became fully human to achieve salvation for all of us mortals brought grace and truth, and he called sexuality into being. During one of my sermons on heaven, I asked, "Is there sex in heaven? "Sexuality is the most exciting sides of the life God created for our happiness. Our sexuality will be enhanced and glorified in the perfect heavenly Kingdom as it is a gift of God for our brief time on earth.

The church itself should not remain silence, but we should sing the praises of sexuality most loudly. The church's faith includes getting together with Jesus Christ who has "broken the dividing wall of hostility," as we discover in Ephesians 2:14. Our time in history has brought devastating and death-dealing hostility between men and women.

The grace of God can enable both sexes to become a mysteriously wonderful drive toward personal communion. Acting out of grace can the church can help heal the distortions of sexuality so that the spiritual power of sexuality can come back to where it belongs.

When we are living according to the highest vales of the true self, we are expressing the best version of ourselves. When we know and claim Jesus as our savior, we are to come as a child. We find an example of joy with which the baby addresses life. In a child, we see the essence of ourselves. It is a spark of divinity, the seed of

God's saving grace. As children, we hear the cultural voices of some parents, yelling "Stop laughing so loudly. You are going to wake up daddy. Stop running fast. you are going to get hurt. Stop that daydreaming and pay attention. Now stop touching yourself down there. There is nothing to get upset or sad about. Self-doubts enter the inner child. Year after year, in each development in the human cycle, we begin to be taught and to choose what others define as good or bad. We then follow the herd and discount our own direct experiences. Sexuality is a theological issue.

Faith communities must become an effective partner in the understanding of Christ's incarnation and ours. This is especially essential to youth. There is a distinction between sex and sexuality. Sex refers to the biological-based need for procreation and body pleasure. Sexuality is defined much broader that goes beyond sex. It does not necessarily involve genital sex. Of course, a total disconnection of these two concepts is impossible. So, the Church must convey this theological issue. The Church has a voice as the hermeneutical agent and space in which a theological understanding of sex and sexuality facilitated to youth as an alternative voice is heard.

The term "youth" was invented after the Industrial Revolution. Before that children and youth were part of the working community. That term "adolescence" is not a disease, but was first used in the early 1900's. That is the reason a subculture emerged. Schools brought a surge in youth culture. This subculture gave young people identity. Now there was opportunity for youth to experience a sense of social reality that is independent and different from the adult culture into which they were born. Youth culture is never static. It changes with each generation.

Youth culture must be understood through language, slang, tattoos, clothing style, body marks, unusual colors of hair, music, art, role models, movies and television. The Church must take time to understand the worldview of youth. Several seminaries such as Princeton and Yale give ministry to youth a high priority.

Youth culture is understood as a product of society. This leads to a diversity of attitudes toward sex than has ever been in the past.

Youth choices relate to the quest for personal fulfillment and emotional happiness as goals for human existence. Our media-saturated atmosphere is in their daily lives. Older people did not grow up with computers, and some vow to never try it. My grandson before age two, would crawl upon a chair, push the on button and type in whatever he could think of, many times PBS. org.

Pornography has far reaching consequences for children and teens. Young people rely on media for information and education on sexual matters, because it is not discussed in homes or churches. Most youth know more about how to perform sex with all its variety much more than anyone in the culture.

Few writers have addressed the place of spirituality in affecting youth attitudes and behavior. One reason the Church is silent is the complex environment, such as the sexuality of single adults, multitudes of pregnancy of youth. Church teaching by all denominations and the actual practices of clergy lead to confusion. Ordination is granted without regard or concern about the morality of those whose sexual practices are never considered by boards of ordination.

Despite the silence of the Church, there is open discussion on sexual issues. Culture and church authority have eroded just when there is now desperate need to express sexuality. There is a tendency to emphasize the difficulties and the differences on this issue. Church and society neglect the things on which there is some clarity mostly financed by parts of the population that promote their agenda. The church must be creative to become meaningful partners in the discourse on sex and sexuality with today's church culture, government, and the distorted views expressed.

Sexual education without an accompanying moral focus does not give the desired and best outcome for youth and the faith communities.

Churches must develop new and fresh dissemination. There are platforms including youth groups, lessons, and sermons in which a space can be created for youth and adults to find biblical guidelines to gain an effective understanding about sex and sexuality. Questions need to be asked and answered. Our spiritual places must not bring confusion. That expected confusion is not the same as rejection for those people who make a choice to understand themselves, God and other people. Church is one of the few safe places to talk about life issues including sexuality in a responsible way. The environment for this has a foundation that nobody is to blame, but everybody is responsible.

This serious talk in dialogue with youth is much more effective than telling them what to do. Youths are equal human beings. Youth are not less human than older adults. Youth is not problem to be solved but a spiritual life mystery that comes out in stories that need to be listened to and appreciated. The open conversation is important. The outcome of the process depends on this approach.

Only when the Word becomes flesh can the biggest part of our creation be appreciated as a normal part of our human being and cannot be suppressed or ignored. The church and the culture moralizes sexuality. The Word of God does not do that at all. Sexuality is a spiritual issue as it can be described as the longing for one another. Sexuality is a positive and joy giving gift, not something designed to prick guilt and shame. Sex involves our total being. The risky behavior of people at every age, such as engaging in intercourse at too young times, even among 11-13-year-old. Pre-teens and teens need clarity and insight on the responsibility of being in the image of God as a sexual being. Faith communities must help. The emphasis our culture focuses on today is on personal pleasure and selfish momentary delight. The Church has an alternative message of discipline, sacrifice, and love for others who are our neighbors.

Our lives depend on respecting ourselves and others in expressing and enjoying our sexuality. Sex is not an act just for pleasure without commitment and love.

The church should never take the place of parents, but needs to support the parents' role as the primary educators of youth. Parents must reserve quality time for their children to create a local, safe place where youth have the courage and opportunity to ask about sex and sexuality. The church and our seminaries need to revisit their theology of sexuality.

Hundreds of church theologians have sought to understand the divinity of Jesus. We know that Jesus was fully human, because if we could not believe that, we would undermine what incarnation means. Jesus was fully human. Jesus did not know everything. On at least one instance, Jesus could not do miracles because there was such lack of faith. He prayed to God. He got sick. Jesus got hungry and thirsty. He would get excited and depressed. He enjoyed a glass of wine. God coming to live on earth reaffirms all life and each life with all the possibilities. Some still do not believe that Christ was fully human. Why are we afraid to go deeper into the mystery of the incarnation? The human Jesus came to enable each of us to be fully human also. In this life, we are called to become transformed into the image of Christ. God entered human life to restore in us the divine image in which we were created.

That divine Word is seeking to become incarnate in us. He inhibits the reality of our flesh and blood in our life. Jesus said that we are the light of the world. The incarnate Word offers us the power to become children of God. We have a God-given capacity to love and to serve and to create, and to convey wisdom, to enjoy all of life and to make all things beautiful. In every area of lives, big and small, including the big one sexuality. The human Jesus opens each one of us to live a grace filled life to become fully human, fully divine, and fully free.

Everything is in Christ, the Eternal Logos, gives a glimpse of what once was in Eden and shall be again. As we interact with the larger society, and add our voice with Christ living inside us in our entire humanness, the Church and all who were created by God, will discover grace and truth in our journey. The Word made flesh makes it all possible.

Chapter Twelve

Positive Messages the Church Needs to Share on Sexuality

Why is sex so fascinating? Why pay attention to what the churches share about sexuality and sex? This fascination points us to a spiritual dimension. Lovers say they "worship" their beloved. They say, "Take me to heaven." A man describes his woman as a "goddess." So, all people use spiritual or religious language when sharing information about sexuality.

During psychotherapy or pastoral counseling therapists tell us that when people bring up sexual questions, they are always religious questions. When clients bring up religious questions, they invariably turn out to have roots in sex. Sex and religion have been difficult to separate. It is so unhealthy to disassociate sex and spirituality. So, when the Church speaks on sexuality, this is not religion or spirituality muscling in on a subject where the churches have no place, but a conversation where the church has always belonged.

People of every age have had to struggle with numerous competing messages concerning sex and sexuality. Most of them are not accurate. We have realized that we must take the responsibility to understand sexuality as God intended it. The church must help the world reconcile their understanding of sex with guidance from the Scripture. What messages about sexuality would you need to hear from the church?

In my research and interviews in preparation for this book, I received insight on the possibilities.

Several wanted to know about God's design for oneness. This topic has been presented at the National Family Life Conferences sponsored by Campus Crusade. Scriptural basis was Ephesians 5:31-32, "Therefore a man shall leave his father and mother and be united to his wife, and the two shall become one flesh. This mystery is profound, and I am saying that it refers to Christ and his church."

The church needs to hear that Paul is giving an example from Genesis to show the relationship of Christ to his bride, the church. They desperately need to understand that becoming one flesh in marriage is life giving, uniting a man and a woman in body, mind, and spirit.

Another message the church needs to convey is that sex was designed by God for pleasure. So much assurance can be taught from the Song of Solomon. In chapter seven, verse six and verse ten reads, "How beautiful and pleasant you are, my loved one, with all your delights. I am my beloved's and his desire is for me." Sex is to be mutually satisfying. Sometimes the love making brings such joy that it coats the person's body and spirit forever. It is an example of God's gift of sexuality.

Ministers have a unique role in understanding that God anatomically designed the female and male bodies with sensitive erogenous zones that when stimulated, result in a passionate climax of one flesh together.

Another suggested coming from singles and those now married is that status does not change the fact that we are called to be pure before the Lord. Jesus said in the Sermon on the Mount, "Blessed are the pure in heart, for they shall see God." Matthew 5:8. Breaking the silence requires a major shift in our culture when he speak about becoming and continuing to be pure. We must stop saying purity is a fear-based, legalistic teaching regarding how we are to behave both before and after marriage. To know this guide to happiness and joy means obedience to God and the fruit of self-control. This message can only be conveyed by grace as demonstrated in our lives as the result of our love relationship with our Creator.

Another subject that couples say would change the climate is that waiting to have sex until you are married does not automatically make your sex life passionate, but it is a skill you can grow in. As the church creates this shameful silent culture, we silence the ones who need to talk. The rejection and shame piles so high and deep, those who struggle feel like they can never ask for guidance. In my interviews, I heard multitudes of horror stories from Christian couples and others. So many beautiful people who saved sex for marriage enter in it with too high, unrealistic expectations. The church's message is that because they honored God by abstaining from sex until marriage will be rewarded even at the ultimate first experience.

This can be a damaging assumption. It's just not true and should not be expected. The first time is your first time. Couples can and will grow to become the best, most passionate lovers. Sex is not the only gift we have for each other in marriage.

Another message people say they need is that there is hope, whatever ways we have missed the mark, and whatever our struggles are. In Galatians 5:1, Paul wrote, "For freedom Christ has set us free; stand firm, therefore, and do not submit again to the yoke of slavery." God offers unconditional love, abundant life, and grace upon grace.

Anyone living today has more access to internet pornography, sensual media, advertisements, and information on sex than ever in the history of humankind. Some of the messages from the church are not bad, just perhaps not deep enough or not filled with understanding and compassion. In my research, two slogans they say are most annoying and not helpful are "modest is hottest" true love waits," or "just say no." This message develops a negative, condemning connotation towards sexuality.

Several young females at a *True Love Waits* conference would say, "Yeah, true love waits for the junior or senior year of high school." Young people do share stories of their sexual experiences. They don desire that in the church, people will give reliable and accurate information. With few exceptions youth report how uncomfortable and inexperienced adults could not give a healthy biblical perspective.

A church can break the silence with a weekend with junior high youth. During this time, we can encourage and allow them to ask questions they Have about their sexuality. For most parents, this is a scary thought. Now Church, ask, "If they do not obtain this information from us, who will they get it from? "

One young professional woman said she wanted some specifics about designing a time to talk with kids from 12 to 15 years old. Go for basic questions such as "What is sex?" Tell them that every sexuality activity may not be directly classified as sex. Sexual experience begins with physical touch, hugging, holding hands, or kissing. Sex then can proceed to more intimate acts.

"What does God say about sex?" Tell them that God is the creator of sex and that God intends it for our life happiness and joy. Remind them that God gives us specific boundaries to keep the beauty in, not to keep the fun stuff out.

"What is sexting? "Sexting involves sending nude pictures or sexy videos of oneself via instant messaging or text messaging.

Another question might be, "What are sexually transmitted diseases? "Every hour in the United States, more than 500 teens contract a sexually transmitted disease. Questions about intercourse, oral sex, pornography, and these are not all the questions junior high kids are interested in.

It is spiritually healthy to say, "I don't know," when you don't know the best way to answer a question. Tell them that you will find an answer and get back to them. Be sure you do just that.

Your church is to be congratulated for facing awkward conversations with courage. You will have done God's will in doing what you have the power to do to help your middle school or junior high youth to enjoy a healthy understanding of sex. During high school, and especially when youth enter college or their first work experience, their curiosity naturally involves questions to married friends about what to expect on the wedding night. Even in preparation sessions before the wedding, ministers do not share the reality and the expectations that couples want to know.

Pastors have reported that more than half the marriages they conduct ceremonies for are with couples who are already pregnant. That fact has been true for many years. And most ordained ministers have struggled with their own theology of sexuality.

When any congregation lives out their beliefs that sexual sin is the worst kind, we stifle evangelism, as our ignorance and silence hinders people who are honestly seeking for God. Many church buildings are open between 11 and 12 noon. So, we outright exclude possible converts from our community. The ethic of younger people who did not grow up in a church family has a significantly different sexual ethic from what guidance they would receive from a biblical foundation. They seek guidance from graphic sex manuals, magazines with glossed-up photographs of naked people, and of course internet porn. They see nothing more seductive than living together outside of marriage. Many have short-term relationships or one-nightstands. They never have a moral thought about it.

What specifically do people speak about when the church breaks the silence? One struggling woman said, "I remember the look of people in the sanctuary when I talked about my infidelity in my marriage. I told about the freedom God has brought me. My testimony today, after the church enabled my soul and marriage to be healed, is priceless. The shock of the difficult truth caused shock in whole bodies, as the truth set me free. God gave me complete forgiveness and with my husband as well. God's mercy never stops at the bedroom door."

A Christian physician noted, "Shame is a part of what makes sexual sin and its consequences so destructive. Anything we can do in the church to encourage people to share their truth, to validate people's stories, and to undermine the power of shame will revolutionize the world."

A Midwestern farmer said, "The shame culture around anything having to do with sex keeps victims of sex crimes from reporting and speaking out. If the church still gives the message that sexual behaviors are shameful, it will remain a tool of coercion and power for sexual abuse, sex traffickers, and those who distort something that brings joy. More people need to know about that."

Only the church can fully explain how God-given sexuality exists in a fallen world. If the earth was populated with only perfect people, we would have the most emotionally and spiritual satisfaction, including the highest experience of joy that we could imagine.

But, sexuality has not been unscathed by sin. No person lives without the thorns that come from memories of our past experiences. Unfortunately, only lies abound about the struggles that plague our marriages.

So, love is impacted by those lies. God alone can transform couples and singles to the joy-filled sexual lives we were designed for by God.

For hundreds of years, the world has tried everything to rid itself of the Christian ethic on sexuality. Our task today is to reclaim sexuality.

Bible studies can help educate in men's or women's groups. Even if you and your church are veterans of Bible studies, one on sexual intimacy may be a little bit intimidating. This topic has not been addressed openly in the past. With sensitivity and candor, and with a discreet and delicate attitude, the Church can address the most intimate and pressing questions within framework of respect, sensitivity, and authenticity.

Deepening our sexual intimacy will be a small part for the church to share all aspects that lead to the highest happiness. Read the passages from Song of Songs 4:9-11 and Proverbs 5:18-19 in a Bible study for couples.

Perhaps the following areas could be helpful. For a positive beginning, ask them to say one thing about our sex life we enjoy now is. Following this discussion ask just what areas do we need to talk about to deepen our sexual intimacy. In a spiritual setting, areas might be positive anticipation, romantic atmosphere, tender words, non-sexual touching, more time for making love, initiation of lovemaking, greater variety, deeper responsiveness, clearing the air about a concern, or any other topic.

God and his people desire us all to rebuild and reclaim the beautiful gift of sexuality. Many stay desperate for the hope of intimacy to be rekindled. Millions living within the steeples of our churches are limping with deep wounds from broken trust or sexual abuse.

During my years of ministry with family therapy and Family Life Conferences and retreats, I have learned that most couples struggle with misunderstanding, selfishness, sexual temptation, communication difficulties and mistakes from their past. Wounds from the past may be re-opened. This can be part of God's healing journey for you. God cares deeply about our souls and the wounds that we have been carrying around in our heads for many years.

One text that is misused to justify sexual rights is I Corinthians 7:2-5. The context of this scripture is about mutual pleasure and satisfaction. The wife is not the property of her husband. Sex is not his right and her obligation. My interpretation of Paul is that husband and wife belong to each other and the sex bed or cherished place for private intimacy is for meeting each other's sexual needs. This word is not about demanding or selfish taking. The emphasis is concerning giving of oneself and of mutual responsibility.

Passion never just happens. Experiencing joy in sex must be pursued, prayed for, sought after, and be taught. The most dedicated Christian gets stuck when passion, romance, and intimacy are issues that block out the highest happiness. There are lonely nights when a woman and a man cry themselves to sleep, drowning in isolation, while their lover slumbers in a distant land while lying next to the joyless person.

Most men do not marry a princess bride. Also, women never marry the perfect man of her dreams. They enable each other through the Lord to become the best versions of themselves.

A wise old monk who had never married at Conception Abbey during a retreat said, "Listen to her. Laugh with her. Encourage her. Give her jewelry. Buy her flowers. Dine her. Wine her. Smile at her. Cuddle with her. Hold her. Write love letters to her. Cry with her. Believe in her. Compliment her. Pray with her. Hold her hand. Go to the moon and back for her."

Greg Alexander, the regional minister for the Christian Church (Disciples of Christ) in Kentucky, held a men's weekend in Nebraska on "Becoming the Man God Calls Me to Be." He noted the deep need for companionship and friendship as deep soul needs for men.

Our entire life is God's artwork. Each person on earth has been given talents and skills for their purpose. We must teach the world to be apprentices of Jesus. If churches focused on Jesus, we would stop treating sexual issues as a personal choice, where sex can be easily turned on and off like a light-switch. Only then will the church begin to create safe places where people can share their burdens with each other and discover that they are not alone.

We all come to a discussion of sexuality carrying prejudices. However closed-minded or open-minded we are, each brings prior commitments to our consideration on this subject. Our prejudices are shaped by our culture and society in which we belong, and by our own personal histories. Our society including spiritual places shape our beliefs about what behaviors are tolerable, accepted, or normal. This is such a dangerous and powerful thing when assumptions are unexamined.

In our day, the movies, magazines, radio, television, soap operas, plays, novels, blogs, and videos all tell stories about people's lives, and in this telling, they established values by explicit disapproval or approval, more often by the silence that assumes a behavior is acceptable.

Powers for evil and powers for good condition our response to communication and thinking about this human gift. Those who are reading this book carries a history of experience or inexperience, of delight and times of joy, or disappointment. Readers come to this subject as participants in the subject, not as objective observers. We receive knowledge about sexuality within sexuality, as sexual beings. Only by participation can we know the existential truth.

Chapter Thirteen

Jesus Ministered to All People

Jesus associated with, ate and drank with the most scorned and lowly persons during his living in a human earthly body. The New Testament tells the stories of a few such as a mentally ill man, prostitutes, adulterous, rich, poor, young, old, sick or well.

When Jesus told the story of the Good Samaritan he was showing how much the Father loved everybody. In today's impending crises in some church groups, Jesus might have used a gay man instead of a Samaritan.

We have found homosexuality, transgender sex, autoerotic, bisexual, or polyamorous sex to be extremely difficult to even think about.

The image that many of us conjure up in our imaginations is the varying physical expression of love between a same sex couple. Exaggeration sand stigmatized visualizations stir up fear and hatred.

No discussion of sex can be divorced from a theology of human sexuality. Sexual union is ordained by God and is pronounced as "very good." People who struggle with same sex desire do not have lower value in the eyes of God.

Intercommunion between male and female has a physical component. Male and female organs are part of God's creation. These organs are subject to a higher understanding of the nature and purpose of humankind. Pleasure is an important part of sexual unions.

In most theologies of sexuality, sex exists for more than pleasure. Sex is necessary for the procreation of humans, deeper knowledge of one's spouse, and a love commitment towards one's spouse and other people. The sexual dimension of life replicates the creative work of God in the world. After years of study on sexuality and being a therapist and a pastoral counselor, I must say the awareness of the spiritual aspects has become quite dim. Scholars and theologians define human beings by their sexual desires, but human relationships are created and nurtured, and are channels through which God accomplishes his divine purposes.

God loves all human kind. Christ's love was selfless. Any sexual expression that is not based on self-giving, self-emptying, committed, and creative love is impure. This will eventually become self-centered, manipulative, and degrading. Love is centered on the good and supportive care. God's love is never self-centered, rude, crude, or casual.

Not so many years ago, homosexual orientation was listed as a mental disorder and a mortal sin. Today's therapists cite no such diagnosis.

The Church Fathers did not know anything about the terminology of modern psychology. They used the term "passions" to describe bodily dispositions. Passionate thoughts come involuntarily and suddenly. Christian standards of conduct exist irrespective of sexual orientation. When a heterosexual decides that they can benefit from my coaching or therapy, I try to show that all people have passions or inclinations toward sexual activity outside of marriage with multiple women. The same goes for women. All Christ-centered people are called to overcome these as spiritual afflictions.

To the homosexual who trusts me in "soul-healing, "I use the same questions and techniques, and I suggest same sex clients have the same kind of passion and inclinations. It is a difficult struggle for any human sexual expressions, but with God's grace, all things are possible.

There is absolutely no good research that indicates sexual orientation can be changed. I must declare that none of my clinical or pastoral work in this area would meet any standard of scientific research.

Jesus asked, "Who is our neighbor? "All humankind must be included in our circles. Clearly, this is a festering subject for the Church and society.

Whatever your sexual orientation is, the Church must seek to be a community where all people are treated with respect, grace, justice, and understanding and humility in the Spirit of Jesus. We are aware of the complexity of current issues. Christ's message must be shared with humility, prayerfulness, and courage. The most effective overarching conversations is that homosexual orientation is not a sin nor a mental illness.

The Fall affects all people and still corrupts all relationships. God loves all people unconditionally and unreservedly. In Christ, we can be compassionating to those who sin by misusing our gift of sexuality. God offers forgiveness and grace when we sin by misusing or distorting our sexuality. According to all we have carefully researched and asked God for guidance, sexual behavior is chosen. Sexual orientation is not a choice.

Jesus and his Church need to be aware that almost everybody's love language includes physical touch. When we speak in hatred and voyeuristic fixation about how people express love hinders us from serving all the people. "The least of these" in Jesus' world had chosen or found themselves in activities or occupations distained by the majority. Lifestyle choices put them in disrepute.

If Jesus loved those who lived in unpopular circumstances created by their own free will, would he not have loved those born with identities beyond their choice?

If we comb through the Bible to find answers, it was Paul not Jesus whoever recorded how he felt about homosexuality. The Bible stands outside and above every culture. It is a book for all time and all times because it does not claim to speak to only one culture, time, and place.

In our "talk" we will use the Bible and do research to support what our minds have already decided. We will do interviews and read books by people who agree with our opinion.

Homosexuals meet ministers such as the late Fred Phelps, pastor of Westboro Baptist Church in Topeka, Kansas, who used the church to show condemnation for homosexuals with trips to graveyards to stir hatred at their funerals. So homosexual oriented people assume that all Christians must be that way. Some assume God must be that way. If the only church people they know are angry at them, then God must hate them as well.

When the Olin T. Binkley Memorial Baptist Church in Chapel Hill, North Carolina gave a young gay man a license to preach, the church was divided. They loved this young seminarian, but they had a long-standing belief that homosexuality was a sin. They prayed together. They studied the Bible together. And they talked a lot to discern the movement of the Holy Spirit in this matter.

They saw the need to bear with one another with Christ-like love. They confessed the arrogance of their certitude. They saw the need to love each person as a child of God. They then vowed to break the code of silence and secrecy. They asked homosexual people about the pain of exclusion that they felt in being cast out, left out, and shut out from the church.

With this courageous and controversial decision, they received a firestorm of threats, hate messages, and exclusion from the Southern Baptist Convention. The church reacted not defensively or with like rudeness, but they extended their way to other churches. Some listened and changed their long-held views. The code of silence is deadly. Denominations are divided. In the United States, congregation by congregation agreed to have the "talk" openly, pray together, reason together, and even agree to disagree. No matter where a person attends church, the church needs to give hurting people the opportunity to move out of hate and judgment.

Breaking the silence is simple. Sit down with people, one by one and pray with them. Listen to their struggles. Be open to the fact that it will take generations many years to find God's will. The journey is for all of us. All people are offered release from sin and guilt and are in Christ loving and serving their neighbors.

Breaking the silence will create anxiety. Good people are feeling that they had been dismissed as being homophobic when you are just trying to say and do is to be faithful to the Word of God as you understand it. Most of us have agreed that homosexuality is sin. We have all heard distorted views of sexuality in sermons, lessons, and books published by publishing houses of our various denominations, I cannot imagine a Christian church without these brothers and sisters not being part of our church.

Every seasoned Christian has reeled to the so-called sexual revolution and the rampant sexual distortion of our culture. And we ache from the crumbling of stable family relationships. Some will not consider any dialogue unless their own son or daughter reveals that they are homosexual. With the priesthood of every believer, we will not move anybody by telling people what a spiritual thinking Christian should believe. No person can be inerrant sure of the mind of God on any subject. People can read and interpret the very same scriptures with vastly different perspectives. We may look to the scholars at Yale, Harvard, Vanderbilt, denominational seminaries, Bible colleges, or diploma mills for assurance, clarification and help. But these places for learning do not agree with each other any more than ordinary church people can come to a solution.

In my pastoral appointments and calls in several denominations, I have struggled with the fundamental, literal, King James Version believing, but sincere followers of Christ who speak out of defense of their interpretation of the Word of God. Some have even yelled at me as they say, I will never welcome gays unless they change.

Many gay believers have wept in my home or church study as they talk about shuffling from one church to another, looking for a place where they can belong, a place to grow deeper in their relationship with Jesus, and to use their gifts in the service of Christ.

Christians will never see everything with total agreement. If there were only two church members in a parish, they would hold disagreements. In the story of the early church as written in the Acts of the Apostles, there were big disagreements. The church leaders really tried to convince each other to see things from their viewpoint. They appeared free to teach their beliefs without fear of punishment. They had the humility to listen to each other. Peter was given a dream to help him see the place of gentiles in the Kingdom of God. Unlike most of our denominations today, they respected other Christians. They believed in what we have called "the priesthood of every believer," knowing that each Christian was attempting to be true to the Holy Scriptures and to growing up to be a healthy community.

The main question is how we are making Jesus Christ lord of our lives? There is no place for adultery or promiscuity, for using another person for pleasure, distorting God's gift of sexuality, regardless of orientation.

Why has the issue of homosexuality become "the" issue in many congregations and denominations? Why are we now ordaining and giving preference to those with homosexual leanings? Why are so many sermons on any part of the Bible twisted to be about the arguments against or for proper human sexuality?

Did subjects like salvation, spirituality, fruit of the Spirit, war, greed, drugs, poverty, money, prayer, or the environment somehow get crowded out? So, the church is left with no positive arguments. Bewilderment is not an argument. Impatience or meanness is not a healthy witness. If the Church continues to have nothing to say, then they cannot be shocked that these issues are being settled by others who have a whole lot to say. The church struggles with the Bible's injunctions that discipleship is about conforming the world to the Bible, not conforming the Bibelot one's world.

The question we could ask both or many sides is "Can the Church demonstrate to the community that the main concern is to be faithful to God as historically revealed in Christ, rather than simply to take up the fashionable cause of the moment? "

In most denominations, there is a tendency toward polite tolerance. So, the people run away, keep silence, and go off into separate congregations. The congregations are then consistent on their theology and cultural opinions. So, they feel safe in knowing that they never must meet somebody that they ever disagree with on their version of the truth.

Church should be a way of continuing conversation with God and one another. Before the word Christian was used, we were called "followers of the Way." The Way was paved with sharing joy, praying, seeking, giving thanks, sharing bread, receiving blessings, and renewing its mission. Jesus made this reconciliation possible. The good news of the gospel is that Christ has broken down the dividing wall of hostility. See Ephesians 2:14.

If the Church continues to not talk to each other, we are communicating that the gospel is a lie, and not filled with grace and truth.

God made all people for relationship. We are all sinners, every single one. We all do damage to relationships. We all struggle with relationships. We all struggle with loneliness. Our goal in life is to be relationally fulfilled. Weal can use help and guidance. We all crave the moments of joy. And all of us need the grace of Christ that we hope will become real in this fellowship for all the people of the world.

Practical Applications

Chapter One

Breaking the Silence About Our Sexual Lives

Do you think sex is an impulse that is difficult to control?

Is sex natural and simple? Do you just have to let yourself go?

Chapter Two

What Do We Mean When We Say, "I Love You"

Why is it so difficult to define the words for love?

How does love change when there is anger and conflict?

What are the Greek words for love?

Chapter Three

Let Us Rejoice and Be Glad in It

Can you recall a time when you experienced sex as a joy?

Are you aware of sex trafficking in your own town or neighborhood?

How does exploitation of sex shrink the views we create about sex?

Chapter Four

It's Time to Have the Talk with the Church

Why do you think most churches are silence about sexuality?

What are some of the sex distortions or lies you have heard in church?

Where do most children and youth hear about sex and sexuality?

What do you share with high school and college students?

Chapter Five

When Did I Get to Be 75 When I Feel Like 25?

How do you visualize older adult couples enjoying sexuality?

In your experience does our culture disregard older women?

How do older people think and do to be attractive?

Can the second half of life be a radiant time with grace?

Chapter Six

The Silence and the Shame of Sexual Violence in the Church

Why is there so much sexual violence and rape in college? What can the church and campus ministry support campus sexuality?

Are males, especially athletes, treated different concerning sexual sin?

How did we get the idea that sex abuse only happens with Catholics?

Chapter Seven

He Had Sex with Someone Else

How do people who are faithful to their marital vows avoid adultery?

What does fulfillment in sex look like?

How does fantasy concerning sex and love affect couples?

Chapter Eight

Silence and the Continuing Sexual Revolution

Why did the sexual revolutions of the 20's and 60's take place?

How is the sexual revolution continuing today?

Chapter Nine

Has God Picked Someone Special for Me to Marry?

How would you answer this question from your children?

What did Jesus mean by "no marriage in heaven? "

What is the difference between love and lust?

Would you fall in love with you?

Chapter Ten

Feeling Life: Sexuality and Joy

Do you think Harry Hollis' prayer could be used in a church?

How does the cultural church show they are anti-sexuality?

Does every sexual experience bring deep joy?

Chapter Eleven

"The Word Became Flesh"

Why is it so hard for us to believe that Jesus came in a body just like ours?

What do we mean by "sexual freedom" in Christ?

What difference does the incarnation of Jesus make in a body theology?

Has this book deepened and stretched your incarnation understanding?

How can we improve the dialogue with youth?

Chapter Twelve

Positive Messages the Church Needs to Share on Sexuality

How does media, sexting, books, and magazines conflict with truth?

What can we say or not say in the church's message about sexuality? Why is there such a lack of extraordinary sex after marriage?

James McReynolds

How can we develop passionate sex within marriage?

How does our ignorance and silence stifle evangelism?

Chapter Thirteen

Jesus Ministered to All People

How would you describe your theology of sexuality?

Have your views of sexuality changed by your study and experience?

Can you relate to the issues of Olin T. Binky Baptist Church?

What do you think Jesus would do in ministry to all people?

Afterword

Congratulations, Jim! You have opened a can of worms urgently begging to be opened, now that our society at large has broken out of the straitjacket imposed upon it by the church and our long centuries of fear and prejudice. There is nothing more connected to life itself than sexuality, and Christianity, from its earliest days until now, has almost always tried to cram it into a box and store it in a corner of the room instead of recognizing how basic it is to all existence and treating it therefore as a precious gift from God.

Like you, I grew up in the Southern Baptist church in an era when sex was almost always regarded as an unmentionable threat in every parlor, board room, school house, and, yes, even the corridors of the church itself. Banned from open discussion, it especially lurked just beneath the surface of every series of evangelical services I ever attended. The more sexually attractive the evangelist and the special singer imported to lead the music, the bigger the crowds and the more successful the services seemed to be. I remember one extremely popular evangelist who came to hold a revival meeting at the church I attended. Not only was he personally very attractive—he even wore flashy outfits and drove a sexy foreign car—but he delighted in telling stories that verged on being openly sexual or suggestive in nature, and the crowds loved it! Although I was only sixteen or seventeen at the time, I still remember today how frankly embarrassed I was at their public delight in his raunchy tales and off-color innuendoes.

Now, with the open acceptance of gays, lesbians, and transgender persons in all areas of public life, the church is being confronted at last by its long history of narrowness, bias, and neglect on the subject of sex, and we are beginning to realize how unforgivably prejudiced we have been. It is high time for ministers within the Christian tradition to become more accepting and understanding, both of the nature of sex itself and of our potential role in helping to guide public exchanges about the true relatedness of godliness and sexuality.

Hopefully this book will help to convince other pastors and Christian teachers to think more deeply and speak more cogently about the relationship of sex to religion and religion to sex. If we don't become more meaningfully engaged in this public discussion, the church will surely cease to have any relevance for the huge masses of young people brimming with sexuality and ripe for the Christian message in our time.

Acknowledgments

Thanks to Dr. David Russell Tullock, the publisher of Parson's Porch Books, whose ministry has challenged the world for good. David is a noted and polished preacher, writer, and publisher. His educational and spiritual foundation was during his undergraduate studies at Carson-Newman University.

Most "preacher boys," but no "preacher girls," had a fire inside for attending Carson-Newman, a Baptist school which had distinguished graduates. I was an unpolished and immature and insecure Christian. My self-esteem was low. I felt inferior to everybody. Some of my classmates were first class people. Beautiful and polished young women caught my attention. Carson-Newman was a strict and conservative school that held chapel every day for all students. I was shy and introverted, but I lived in the loud and crowded Memorial Hall. The Baptist churches and schools were silent on relationships and sexuality. I never believed it when any woman would say intimate or nice things to me. Even though I had a normal fire for sex and sexuality, I never felt really loved, and I certainly would have been a poor husband with absolutely no experience with sex. I held depression, anger, rejection, and too much ambition to succeed in my calling. I would not be supportive or caring as I did not love myself.

My freshman English professor, Agnes Hull, who gave me grades of plus, but never an A minus, which made a difference to me. Her standard gave less credence to her saying I was her best student. She encouraged me and said I had a poetic soul and a gift for writing.

She would drive me down to First Baptist Church in Knoxville, where Carson-Newman graduate the Rev. Dr. Charles Trentham served as senior pastor. Miss Hull introduced me to Dr. Trentham, who preached on television every Sunday.

His scholarly sermons moved me. The church called me as student pastor of prayer while I was at Carson-Newman. My goal was to serve as a pastor in a church like the First Baptist Church. I did sense that many did not like or appreciate his soft scholarly style.

To my departed mom and dad who encourage me to be faithful. To my wife Laurel, whose love and patience has been the cornerstone of our marriage. To my brothers, David and Edward, all the children and grandchildren who gathered in the Smoky Mountains for a meaningful reunion. To our huge family on both sides who have been bearers of happiness.

To my longtime friend, Dr. John Killinger, my professor during my studies at Vanderbilt University Divinity School. And to so many others who helped me be a communicator of joy to the world.

To my colleagues at the Sunday School Board of the Southern Baptist Convention where I served promoting and writing as a public relations specialist. My parents enrolled me in cradle roll on the Sunday after my birth at the First Baptist Church in Kingsport, Tennessee, where I was delivered for my earthly journey by a physician who was a graduate of Carson-Newman and the University of Tennessee Medical School. Our family moved to Bristol, Tennessee after the war. We lived in a small apartment up over a grocery store, and across the street from Woodlawn Baptist Church. Church was my social life, my spiritual life, and all of life.

To the leaders of the 12 denominations on whose staffs I served and whose insights made me the ecumenical Christian that I am today.

To the regional board of the Christian Church (Disciples of Christ) of Nebraska who honored me with a lovely plaque for my ministry. I was elected as moderator and saw joys and miracles in ten years as pastor of the First Christian Church in Weeping Water, Nebraska. I am now actively retired from the Christian Church (Disciples of Christ) and a retired elder for the Holston Conference of the United Methodist Church.

To all those who came to me for soul-healing psychotherapy, ready articles and books, and heard me preach and teach. And to those who shared with me in my ministry of life coaching and ministry in several retirement centers and care centers.

To all those whose love and support is forever infused in this book and in my brief earthly journey and our shared experiences. You are in the positive videos in my soul.

www.ingramcontent.com/pod-product-compliance
Lightning Source LLC
Chambersburg PA
CBHW052151110526
44591CB00012B/1935